Diving & Snorkeling

Belize

Mark Webster

LONELY PLANET PUBLICATIONS
Melbourne • Oakland • London • Paris

Diving & Snorkeling Belize
- A Lonely Planet Pisces Book

3rd Edition – June 2002
2nd Edition – September 1998
1st Edition – 1990 Gulf Publishing Company

Published by
Lonely Planet Publications Pty Ltd, ABN 36 005 607 983
90 Maribyrnong St., Footscray, Victoria 3011, Australia

Other offices
150 Linden Street, Oakland, California 94607, USA
10a Spring Place, London NW5 3BH, UK
1 rue du Dahomey, 75011 Paris, France

Photographs
by Mark Webster (unless otherwise noted)

Front cover photograph
Diver explores Nurse Shark Ridge, Long Caye,
    Lighthouse Reef, by Mark Webster

Back cover photographs
Aerial view of Blue Hole Natural Monument,
    Lighthouse Reef, by Greg Johnston
Black howler monkey, by Tom Boyden
A diver glides over West Point Wall,
    Turneffe Islands, by Mark Webster

All of the images in this guide are available for
    licensing from **Lonely Planet Images**
www.lonelyplanetimages.com

ISBN 1 74059 047 3

Printed by H&Y Printing Ltd., Hong Kong

Contents

Introduction   **9**

Overview   **11**

    Geography 11

    Geology 12

    History 12

Practicalities   **15**

    Climate 15

    Language 15

    Getting There 16

    Gateway City – Belize City 16

    Getting Around 18

    Entry 19

    Time 19

    Money 19

    Electricity 19

    Weights & Measures 20

    What to Bring 20

    Underwater Photography 20

    Business Hours 21

    Accommodations 21

    Dining & Food 22

    Shopping 22

Activities & Attractions   **23**

    Belize Zoo 23

    Crooked Tree Wildlife Sanctuary 24

    Bermudian Landing Community Baboon Sanctuary 25

    Guanacaste National Park 26

    Gales Point Wildlife Sanctuary 26

    Cockscomb Basin Wildlife Sanctuary 26

    Mayan Ruins 27

Diving Health & Safety 30

Pre-Trip Preparation 31

DAN 32

Medical & Recompression Facilities 32

Diving in Belize 34

Dive Training & Certification 36

Snorkeling 36

Live-Aboards 36

Day Boats 38

Pisces Rating System for Dives & Divers 40

Northern Cayes Dive Sites 42

1 Mexico Rocks 45

2 Statue 46

3 Tres Cocos 47

4 Tackle Box Canyons 48

5 Mermaids' Lair 49

6 Esmarelda 50

7 Boca Ciega 51

8 Cypress Tunnels 51

9 Pillar Coral 52

10 Hol Chan Cut 53

11 Shark-Ray Alley 54

12 Amigos' Wreck 54

13 Coral Canyons 56

14 Stingray Village 56

15 Caye Chapel Reef 57

Middle Cayes Dive Sites 58

16 Faegon's Point 60

17 Faegon's Bluff 61

18 'Cuda Point ('Cuda Scuda) 62

19 Fishy Point 63

20 Turtle's Rest 64

21 Tobacco Cut 64

22 Tobacco Channel. 66

23 Eagle Ray Bowl 66

24 Jack Fish City. 67

25 Coral Monument Canyon. 68

Southern Cayes Dive Sites   69

26 Mosquito Caye South 72

27 Laughing Bird Caye North 73

28 Laughing Bird Caye 74

29 Laughing Bird Caye South 75

30 North Wall 76

31 Silk Cayes (Queen Cayes). 77

32 Silk Cayes Canyons 78

33 Pompion Caye Wall 79

34 Pompion Caye. 80

35 Chub Canyons. 81

Offshore Atolls Dive Sites   82

Turneffe Islands   82

36 Sandy Lane 84

37 Black Coral Wall 85

38 Mini Elbow 86

39 Triple Anchors 87

40 *Sayonara*. 88

41 West Point Wall. 88

42 The Elbow 90

43 Black Beauty 90

Lighthouse Reef   91

44 Blue Hole 93

45 Eagle Ray Wall. 94

46 The Aquarium 95

47 Silver Caves. 96

48 Painted Wall 96

49 Julie's Jungle 98

50 Quebrada 99

51 Long Caye Ridge 100

52 Pete's Palace 101

53 Nurse Shark Ridge 102

54 No Cocos (Tres Cocos) 102

55 Elkhorn Forest 103

56 Half Moon Wall 104

57 Shark Point 106

Glover's Reef   **107**

58 Long Caye Lagoon 110

59 Long Caye Cut 111

60 Long Caye Wall 112

61 Bev's Garden 113

62 The Crack 113

63 The Abyss 114

64 Middle Caye Wall 114

65 The Pinnacles 115

66 West Wall 117

Marine Life   118

Hazardous Marine Life 121

Diving Conservation & Awareness   124

Marine Reserves & Regulations 124

Responsible Diving 126

Listings   128

Telephone Calls 128

Accommodations 128

Diving Services & Resorts 130

Live-Aboards 132

Tourist Offices 132

Index   133

Author

Mark Webster

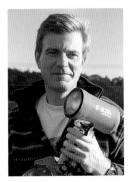

Mark Webster first became interested in underwater photography while working as a commercial diver in the North Sea. Success in international competitions soon followed, including third place overall in the CMAS World Championships of Underwater Photography. Mark writes regularly for scuba diving magazines, and his photos have appeared in many diving, photography and wildlife publications, as well as Lonely Planet's *Diving & Snorkeling Red Sea*. He hosts regular underwater photography workshops in the Red Sea and Indonesia and often makes presentations at trade shows and seminars. Mark's other books include *The Art & Technique of Underwater Photography*, *The Blue* (UNESCO), *Reef Fish & Corals of the Red Sea* and *Diving Guide to Northern Europe*. He lives in southwest England.

From the Author

Lots of preparation goes into writing a dive guide. Local knowledge is especially essential for presenting accurate information. I'd like to thank the following people for their generous help and support: Golda Tillet at the Belize Tourism Board; Mike Cobb at Exotic Caye; Julia Edwards at the Sun Breeze Beach Hotel; Maria Otera at the Radisson Fort George; Hugh Parkey; Lynne Mellone at the Best Western Belize Biltmore Plaza; Maria Vega at the Vega Inn; Kathy Dalton and Dawn Williams at Belize Diving Services; Ghislaine Hoare and Terri Valentine at the Pelican Beach Resort; Elana Pano, Culley Erdman and Lucy Wallingford at Slickrock Adventures; Jim and Kendra Schofield at Off the Wall Dive Shop; Andrew Muha at Tobacco Caye Diving; Risa and Bob Frackman at The Inn at Robert's Grove; Sue Hamilton, Peter Hughes and the crew of *Wave Dancer*.

Finally, I would like to thank my wife, Susanna, for her patience with yet another book, her hours of proofreading and for modeling so willingly and repeatedly underwater.

Photography Notes

Underwater, Mark uses Nikon F90x cameras housed in Subal Miniflex housings with Sea & Sea, Isotta and Subatec strobes. For wide-angle photography he uses 16mm fisheye and 20mm lenses. For macro and close-up photography he prefers 60mm, 105mm and 180mm lenses lit by an Inon flash ring. Topside, he works with the Nikon F90x and a variety of lenses. He prefers Fujichrome and Kodachrome film, particularly Velvia for macro work and Provia or Elitechrome for wide-angle shots.

Contributing Photographers

Mark Webster took most of the photographs in this book. Thanks also to Tom Boyden, John Elk III, Greg Johnston, Michael Lawrence, Andrew Marshall and Leanne Walker, Kevin McDonnell, Carolyn Miller and Tony Wheeler.

From the Publisher

This third edition was published in Lonely Planet's U.S. office under the guidance of Roslyn Bullas, the Pisces Books publishing manager. David Lauterborn edited the text and photos with buddy checks from Roslyn Bullas, Deb Miller and Michael Johnson. Emily Douglas designed the cover, and Gerilyn Attebery designed the interior with assistance from Emily. Navigating the nautical charts was cartographer Rachel Jereb, who created the maps, with assistance from Brad Lodge. U.S. cartography manager Alex Guilbert supervised map production. Lindsay Brown reviewed the Marine Life section for scientific accuracy. Portions of the text were adapted from Lonely Planet's *Belize*.

Pisces Pre-Dive Safety Guidelines

Before embarking on a scuba diving, skin diving or snorkeling trip, carefully consider the following to help ensure a safe and enjoyable experience:

- Possess a current diving certification card from a recognized scuba diving instructional agency (if scuba diving)

- Be sure you are healthy and feel comfortable diving

- Obtain reliable information about physical and environmental conditions at the dive site (e.g., from a reputable local dive operation)

- Be aware of local laws, regulations and etiquette about marine life and environment

- Dive at sites within your experience level; if possible, engage the services of a competent, professionally trained dive instructor or divemaster

Underwater conditions vary significantly from one region, or even site, to another. Seasonal changes can significantly alter site and dive conditions. These differences influence the way divers dress for a dive and what diving techniques they use.

There are special requirements for diving in any area, regardless of location. Before your dive, ask about environmental characteristics that can affect your diving and how trained local divers deal with these considerations.

Warning & Request

Things change—dive site conditions, regulations, topside information. Nothing stays the same for long. Your feedback on this book will be used to help update and improve the next edition. Excerpts from your correspondence may appear in *Planet Talk*, our quarterly newsletter, or *Comet*, our monthly email newsletter. Please let us know if you do not want your letter published or your name acknowledged.

Correspondence can be addressed to:
Lonely Planet Publications
Pisces Books
150 Linden Street
Oakland, CA 94607
email: pisces@lonelyplanet.com

Introduction

The Caribbean boasts many attractions for visiting divers, but only Belize offers the unique topography of the world's second-longest barrier reef and three of the Western Hemisphere's four coral atolls. The waters off this tiny Central American country also contain more than 450 scattered cayes and small islands. Together these features promise an amazing variety of diving, featuring some of the region's most spectacular walls and the impressive Blue Hole, a collapsed underwater cavern made famous during Jacques Cousteau's 1970 expedition to Belize.

Diving fuels much of the country's growing tourism industry. You'll find a range of dive resorts and centers to suit every pocket and preference. Day boats visit the reefs two or three times a day, while live-aboards allow more experienced divers extended excursions to the outlying cayes and offshore atolls. Whatever your experience level, you can choose from a treasure trove of reefs, walls, swim-throughs, caves and atoll lagoons that shelter a dazzling selection of corals, sponges, fish, invertebrates and marine mammals. Snorkelers can indulge their curiosity in the calm shallow waters of the fringing reefs and lagoons.

Travel to and within the country is easy. Several flights a day arrive in Belize City from the continental U.S., connecting arrivals from North and South America and Europe. Transfers to your final destination are by air or water taxi. Your travel itinerary will take you through mainland Belize, an increasingly popular ecotourism destination blessed with stunning wildlife, botanical and archaeological attractions. You'll wonder at the country's flora and fauna, while the fascinating ruins and relics of its Mayan past are well worth an inland excursion. Whether you're looking for world-class dive sites or a variety of topside diversions, Belize has it all.

This guide covers 66 of Belize's most popular sites, including dives in the **Northern Cayes, Middle Cayes, Southern Cayes** and **Offshore Atolls**. You'll find detailed site information, including topography, depth range, recommended diver expertise, highlights and typical marine life you might encounter. The Marine Life section offers a photo gallery of the region's most common vertebrates, invertebrates and hazardous species. Travelers with an interest in cave dives, shore dives, wreck dives or snorkeling sites will find those headings in the index. While not intended to be a stand-alone travel guide, the book also provides practical topside information, an overview of the country's history and culture, and suggested activities and attractions to pass your time between dives.

GREG JOHNSTON

The world's second-longest barrier reef is one of many highlights that draw divers to Belize.

Overview

Flanked by the warm Caribbean Sea, Belize (formerly British Honduras) is nestled along the eastern seaboard of the narrow isthmus that connects North and South America. Mexico lies to the north and Guatemala to the west and south. Almost a third of the country is devoted to the national park system or claims protected status. You'll find thousands of species of flowering plants, orchids and trees, many

ANDREW MARSHALL AND LEANNE WALKER

of which are endemic to the region. The country is also home to more than 500 species of birds and is one of the few remaining places to encounter a jaguar in the wild.

Though Belize's multicultural population numbers less than a quarter of a million, the country welcomes twice that number of tourists annually. Most of the population lives along the coast, mainly in Belize City. This former capital city is built on a low-lying, swampy peninsula. After Hurricane Hattie devastated the city in 1961, the government was relocated inland to Belmopan. However, Belize City quickly recovered and remains the nation's tourism capital and gateway to both the interior and barrier reef.

GREG JOHNSTON

Much of mainland Belize is lushly forested.

Geography

Belize can be broadly divided into two main physiographic regions. The Maya Mountains and their associated basins and plateaus dominate the southwest, capped by Victoria Peak, which rises to 3,675ft (1,120m) in the Cockscomb Basin. Cloaked with primary tropical rainforest, the area boasts an abundant variety of wildlife.

The second region comprises the northern lowlands and the coastal plain. Dotted with lagoons and fed by dozens of rivers and streams, much of the coast is marshy. As you progress inland up north, the terrain changes from mangrove swamps to tropical pine savannas and hardwood forests.

11

Geology

Much of Belize sits atop several varieties of limestone, with the exception of the massive granite intrusion of the Maya Mountains. Although several impressive faults run through the mountains, the country lies outside the main zone of tectonic activity that affects much of Central America. The foothills feature typical limestone karst topography, with numerous sinkholes, caverns and underground streams. These gradually give way to alluvial deposits along the coast.

The shallow coastal plain extends offshore some 15 to 18 miles (24 to 29km) to the coral spine of the Belize Barrier Reef, which parallels most of the 185-mile (300km) coastline. Stretching from Banco Chinchorro in Mexican waters south to neighboring Guatemala and Honduras, the reef follows a fault system, the source of its dramatic seaward walls.

Tectonic activity also formed the foundations of the three atolls (the Turneffe Islands, Lighthouse Reef and Glover's Reef), which lie offshore from the barrier reef. More commonly found in the Indo-Pacific, the classic atoll formation features fringing reefs and low-lying islands that ring placid shallow lagoons.

Belize Barrier Reef

A barrier reef is a continuous coral buttress that forms parallel to a coastline. Unlike a fringing reef, it's separated from land by continuous or interlinked lagoons. The reef itself rises to just below the surface and often caps precipitous walls or drop-offs along its seaward edge.

The 160-mile (260km) Belize Barrier Reef fits this description perfectly and is the second longest of its type in the world (the longest is Australia's Great Barrier Reef). Comprising more than 70 species of hard coral, the reef is home to more than 600 species of fish and invertebrates.

History

Although Belize is now an independent nation, its origins lie with the Mayan Empire, which dominated the Yucatan Peninsula and what is now Central America some 1,300 years ago. At the empire's peak, more than 1 million Maya inhabited its complex cities and temples, forming an advanced society centered on mathematics, astronomy, engineering and art. Exactly why the civilization declined so rapidly after AD 900 is still open for debate, but by the time Christopher Columbus arrived in the Bay of Honduras in 1502, few Maya remained, and many of their cities and temples had already vanished beneath the jungle.

The 1500s marked the start of European world expansion and the exploitation that accompanied it, particularly in the Americas. Though they were the first to claim Belize, the Spanish showed little interest, as the region had few resources and its waters were hazardous to shipping. The lethal barrier reef and string of cayes did, however, attract pirates and privateers over the following century.

TOM BOYDEN

On the Gautemalan border in western Belize, the Chechem Ha caves still hold Mayan relics.

Mostly British, they used this natural cover to pounce on Spanish treasure fleets returning from the New World. Gradually their bases moved ashore, and the expanding timber trade led to establishment of the first settlements. These towns became British by default, with the tacit approval of the British monarchy.

Rivalry between the two nations grew throughout the 16th century and inevitably led to a decisive clash at St. George's Caye on September 10, 1798. The battle raged between a Spanish fleet of 32 ships and the British man-of-war HMS *Merlin*, supported by a handful of sailing boats and gun rafts. Despite being heavily outnumbered, the British force prevailed. It wasn't until 1862, however, that British rule was officially declared, following the signing of a treaty with neighboring Guatemala. The country was named British Honduras.

Two world wars and a sea change in attitudes regarding empire building led to the gradual breakup of the British Empire. In British Honduras internal political pressure built till self-government was granted in 1964. The country was renamed Belize in 1973, and full independence was granted in September 1981. Claiming ownership of certain lands in Belize, Guatemala renewed its threats of invasion, so British troops remained to defend against potential incursions. Finally, in 1992 the newly elected Guatemalan government signed another treaty, and the British largely departed Belize, leaving an indelible mark on its constitution and society.

Today the economy relies on a mixture of resources. Ranches and farms dot the lowlands south and west of Belize City, sugarcane plantations dominate up north, and the timber industry thrives on high ground around the Maya Mountains. Tourism is the other major contributor, boosted by a recent trend toward ecotourism and excursions to Mayan ruins.

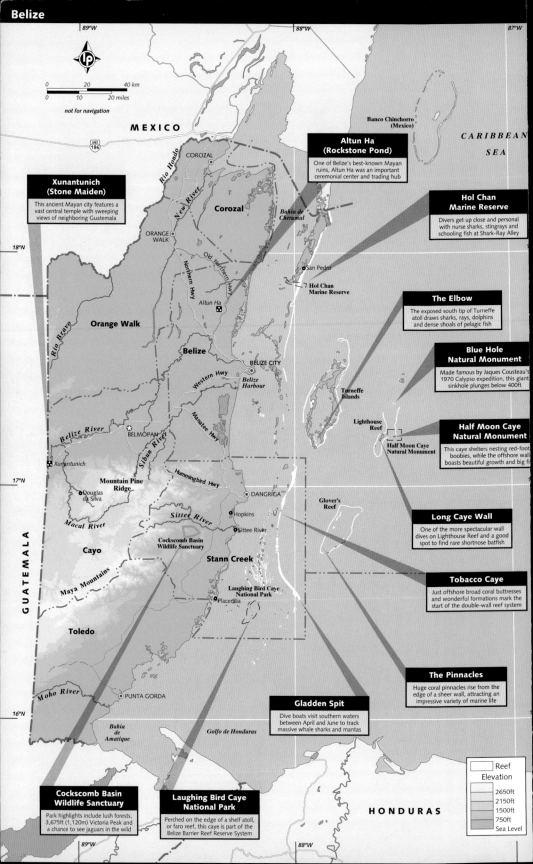

Belize

0 20 40 km
0 10 20 miles

not for navigation

MEXICO

CARIBBEAN SEA

Banco Chinchorro (Mexico)

MEX 186

COROZAL

Altun Ha (Rockstone Pond)
One of Belize's best-known Mayan ruins, Altun Ha was an important ceremonial center and trading hub

Xunantunich (Stone Maiden)
This ancient Mayan city features a vast central temple with sweeping views of neighboring Guatemala

Corozal

Bahía de Chetumal

ORANGE WALK

18°N

San Pedro

Hol Chan Marine Reserve

Hol Chan Marine Reserve
Divers get up close and personal with nurse sharks, stingrays and schooling fish at Shark-Ray Alley

Orange Walk

Altun Ha

The Elbow
The exposed south tip of Turneffe atoll draws sharks, rays, dolphins and dense shoals of pelagic fish

Belize

BELIZE CITY

Belize Harbour

Turneffe Islands

Blue Hole Natural Monument
Made famous by Jaques Cousteau's 1970 Calypso expedition, this giant sinkhole plunges below 400ft

BELMOPAN

Lighthouse Reef

17°N

Half Moon Caye Natural Monument

Half Moon Caye Natural Monument
This caye shelters nesting red-foot boobies, while the offshore wall boasts beautiful growth and big fis

Mountain Pine Ridge

Douglas da Silva

Xunantunich

Long Caye Wall
One of the more spectacular wall dives on Lighthouse Reef and a good spot to find rare shortnose batfish

Glover's Reef

DANGRIGA

Cayo

Hopkins

Sittee River

Cockscomb Basin Wildlife Sanctuary

Stann Creek

Tobacco Caye
Just offshore broad coral buttresses and wonderful formations mark the start of the double-wall reef system

Laughing Bird Caye National Park

Placencia

Toledo

The Pinnacles
Huge coral pinnacles rise from the edge of a sheer wall, attracting an impressive variety of marine life

PUNTA GORDA

16°N

Bahía de Amatique

Golfo de Honduras

Gladden Spit
Dive boats visit southern waters between April and June to track massive whale sharks and mantas

Cockscomb Basin Wildlife Sanctuary
Park highlights include lush forests, 3,675ft (1,120m) Victoria Peak and a chance to see jaguars in the wild

Laughing Bird Caye National Park
Perched on the edge of a shelf atoll, or faro reef, this caye is part of the Belize Barrier Reef Reserve System

HONDURAS

Reef
Elevation

2650ft
2150ft
1500ft
750ft
Sea Level

GUATEMALA

Rio Hondo

New River

Old Northern Hwy

Northern Hwy

Rio Bravo

Belize River

Western Hwy

Manatee Hwy

Sibun River

Hummingbird Hwy

Macal River

Maya Mountains

Moho River

Sittee River

Practicalities

Climate

Belize enjoys pleasant tropical conditions year-round. Temperatures range between 75°F (24°C) in winter and 89°F (32°C) in summer, although easterly trade winds make even the hottest months comfortable along the coast. Annual rainfall approaches 7ft (2m), and sudden brief downpours are common, often followed by blazing sunshine. Late summer is tropical storm season, but hurricanes are rare. In winter months, cold fronts out of North America bring strong northeasterly winds. While short-lived, these are sometimes strong enough to suspend diving on all but the most sheltered reefs.

Diving Conditions

Water temperatures are fairly consistent, varying between 79°F (26°C) in the winter to 84°F (29°C) at the height of summer. Most divers opt to wear a shorty wetsuit or lycra dive skin, though a 2mm full wetsuit is advisable if you're making repeated or extended dives.

Visibility on the barrier reef and atolls is often excellent, reaching more than 100ft (30m), while visibility on shallower nearshore reefs averages between 40 and 65ft (12 and 20m), depending on surface conditions. The tidal range in Belize is generally no greater than 2ft (.6m), so currents are typically mild.

Language

English is the official and most widely spoken language in Belize, although the majority Creoles (descended from African slaves and the early British pirates) also speak a Caribbean patois. People in the tourist industry often switch between the two—if you have trouble understanding, politely repeat your question. Other languages reflect the country's rich racial mix, from mestizos, those of mixed native Indian and European ancestry, to indigenous Maya, who comprise some 10% of the population.

Belizeans reflect a mix of cultures.

Getting There

Most visitors to Belize arrive by plane at Phillip SW Goldson International Airport (BZE), 9 miles (16km) northwest of Belize City. American Airlines, Continental Airlines and Grupo TACA offer direct flights from the continental U.S. Most international flights connect through Dallas, Houston, Miami or Los Angeles.

Connecting flights within Belize are available out of the international airport. Another option is to take a taxi to nearby Municipal Airport (TZA), where flights depart every hour. Bear in mind, however, that this tiny airport only operates during daylight hours—if your inbound flight arrives late, you'll be spending the night in Belize City. Tropic Air and Maya Island Air are the primary local airlines.

If you're visiting Belize as part of a dive package, your tour operator will arrange all transfers.

Domestic flights are available from Belize City to many of the outlying cities and cayes.

Gateway City – Belize City

Although Belize City (population 80,000) is no longer the capital, it remains the gateway to the country. Perched on the tip of a peninsula, the city is bisected by Haulover Creek, a tributary of the Belize River. Down by the harbor is the commercial center, where you'll find the consulates and embassies, major banks, shops and the tourism board offices, which include the visitor information center. Close by are the post office, the BTL Telephone Office and the central taxi stand.

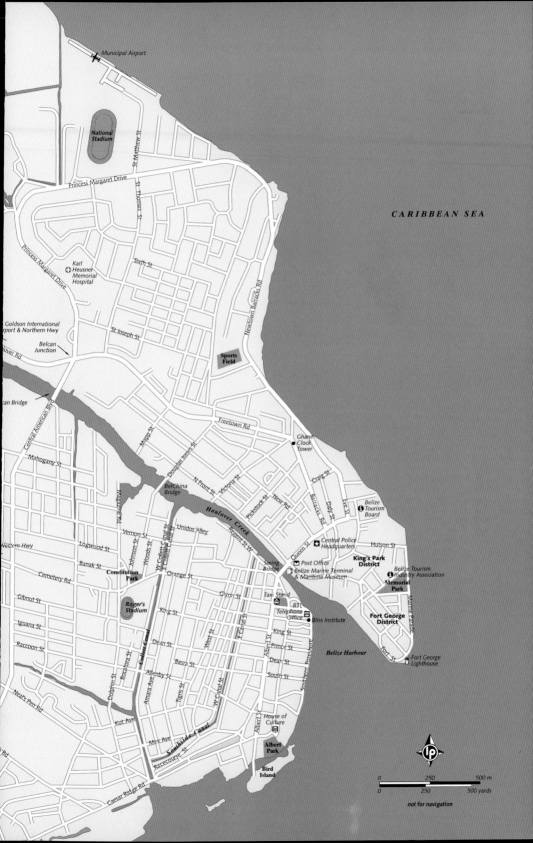

CARIBBEAN SEA

Municipal Airport

National
Stadium

Princess Margaret Drive

Karl
Heusner
Memorial
Hospital

St Matthew St

St Thomas St

Sixth St

Princess Margaret Drive

Goldson International
Airport & Northern Hwy

St Joseph St

Belcan
Junction

Hover Rd

Newtown Barrack Rd

Sports
Field

can Bridge

Central American Blvd

Mahogany St

Mapp St

Douglas Jones St

Freetown Rd

Ghane
Clock
Tower

Western Hwy

Logwood St

Banak St

Cemetery Rd

Gibnut St

Iguana St

Raccoon St

Neal's Pen Rd

Rd

Magazine Rd

Vernon St

Johnson St

Woods St

Constitution
Park

Roger's
Stadium

Dolphin St

Bocatora St

Amara Ave

Allenby St

Kut Ave

Mex Ave

Racecourse St

Caesar Ridge Rd

BelChina
Bridge

N Front St

Victoria St

Haulover Creek

Unidos Alley

W College Hall
E College Canal

Orange St

King St

Dean St

Basra St

Thurn St

W Canal St

Coffeax Canal

Southside Canal

Regent St W

Pickstock St

New Rd

Craig St

Barracks Rd

Daly St

Eve St

Belize
Tourism
Board

Central Police
Headquarters

Hutson St

King's Park
District

Belize Tourism
Industry Association

Memorial
Park

Fort George
District

Marine Parade

Swing
Bridge

Queen St

Post Office

Belize Marine Terminal
& Maritime Museum

Taxi Stand

BTC
Telephone
Office

Bliss Institute

Albert St

King St

Prince St

Dean St

South St

Southern Foreshore

Belize Harbour

Fort St

Fort George
Lighthouse

Glynn St

West St

W Canal St

Albert St

House of
Culture

Albert
Park

Bird
Island

0   250   500 m
0   250   500 yards

not for navigation

Replaced by Belmopan as the country's capital, bustling Belize City remains the tourism hub.

Belize City offers few tourist attractions, although the Swing Bridge, the Bliss Institute, the Maritime Museum and the gardens at the House of Culture are worth a look. Also consider a stroll in the Fort George district, which boasts much of the city's intact colonial architecture.

Getting Around

Taxi service is available throughout Belize City, while tours to surrounding attractions are typically arranged through your hotel or travel agent. For the more adventurous, buses run from Belize City to a variety of destinations both inland and along the southern coast. Watch your luggage carefully, particularly when bags are loaded or unloaded.

Rental cars are available from local and international agencies. Make arrangements at the airport or through your hotel. Although the major routes are largely paved, most other roads are narrow dirt stretches, so consider renting a four-wheel-drive vehicle. Bring a good map, as road signs are few and far between. Another option is to hire a private car and driver.

Water taxis depart several times a day for Ambergris Caye and Caye Caulker from the marine terminal beside the Swing Bridge in Belize City. These trips are in fast open speedboats, so wear a hat and plenty of sunblock and expect to get a little wet.

Tropic Air and Maya Island Air offer domestic routes from both airports in Belize City, flying north and south with stops at the various cayes. Be sure to book ahead, as the plane may not stop at your airport if no passengers are scheduled for pickup. These flights are reliable, reasonably priced and the best option if you're on a tight schedule.

Entry

To enter Belize, citizens of many countries (including the U.S., Canada and the U.K.) must have a valid passport and an onward or return ticket from Belize. Your passport will be stamped with a visitor's permit that's valid for 30 days.

The customs process is generally painless, though officials randomly inspect bags. If you're carrying lots of camera, video or computer equipment, you may be asked to register their serial numbers and value with customs on arrival. To avoid delays, carry a typewritten list of your equipment with your passport. The details will be marked in your passport and checked when you leave Belize.

The current departure tax is US$20—of this US$3.75 goes toward conservation projects. Airports also charge a minimal departure tax for domestic flights.

Time

Belize is on Central Standard Time, six hours behind Greenwich Mean Time (GMT). Daylight saving time is not observed. During standard time, when it's noon in Belize, it's 10am in San Francisco, 1pm in New York, 6pm in London and 5am the following day in Sydney.

Money

The official currency is the Belizean dollar, which still bears Queen Elizabeth's portrait. However, the U.S. dollar is widely used, though you're likely to be given change in Belizean dollars unless you ask. Denominations for coins and notes are similar to U.S. currency. While the exchange rate at banks and hotels varies, most businesses observe a steady unofficial rate of BZ$2 to US$1.

U.S. traveler's checks and major credit cards are widely accepted. Some banks in Belize City have ATMs, though many of these only accept locally issued cards.

Belize levies an 8% value-added tax on retail sales, as well as a 7% tax on hotel rooms, meals and drinks. Tip tour leaders, dive staff and waitstaff at your discretion, though tips need go no higher than 10% of your bill.

Electricity

Electrical current throughout Central and North America is 110 volts, 60Hz AC. Most outlets accept ungrounded plugs with two parallel blades (one slightly larger than the other) or grounded plugs with two parallel blades and a rounded shaft. Bring a travel adapter if necessary. You'll also need a transformer for 240-volt appliances, although live-aboard boats often have an additional 240-volt supply to accommodate European clients.

Weights & Measures

Belize uses both imperial and metric measurements interchangeably. For example, while your rental car speedometer will be in kilometers per hour (km/h), the few road signs still indicate distances in miles.

In this book both imperial and metric measurements are given, except for specific references in dive site descriptions, which are given in imperial units only. Please refer to the conversion chart provided on the inside back cover.

What to Bring

General

Belizeans have a laid-back approach to life, which means you can travel light and pack mostly shorts and T-shirts. Even at upscale hotels in Belize City, casual clothing is acceptable, although you may prefer to have something more formal for dining out. Informality is expected on the island resorts. For windy or wet days you may want to bring a windbreaker, while a sweatshirt should keep you warm after a night dive.

The sun in Belize can be fierce. Factor in the cooling trade winds, and it's easy to get badly sunburned before you realize it. Bring plenty of waterproof sunblock, sunglasses and a wide-brimmed hat. If you plan any inland excursions, pack plenty of insect repellent to keep mosquitoes at bay.

Dive-Related

Don't forget to pack your C-card. Some dive centers may also ask to see your logbook and a certificate of medical eligibility from your doctor, particularly if you're taking any medication or have a condition that might otherwise preclude diving. If you plan to take further certification courses during your vacation, remember to bring passport-sized photos for your C-card.

The quality of dive rental gear in Belize is generally good, but be sure to check equipment thoroughly before you dive. If you're joining a live-aboard and intend to use only their equipment, contact the operator in advance to ensure they have everything you need in your sizes. For the best fit, it's best to bring at least your own wetsuit, mask, snorkel and fins.

It's also advisable to bring a dive computer to monitor your decompression profiles from day to day. Most dive centers rent computers, though you should check in advance.

Underwater Photography

If you'd like to try your hand at underwater photography or videography, it's possible to rent basic camera setups. Some dive centers and live-aboards even offer photography courses. If you're already serious about it, you'll likely bring your own equipment, though rental options exist in the event of a failure. Print film processing is available in Ambergris Caye and Belize City, and both live-aboards offer onboard E6 processing.

You can buy print film and disposable cameras throughout Belize, but if you prefer a particular brand, speed or slide film, then bring your own. This also applies to videotapes and batteries.

Business Hours

Hours vary between the cities and resorts, but most shops open between 8 and 9am, break for lunch, then close between 4 and 6pm. Many of the resort shops and hotel boutiques remain open in the evenings. Businesses close early on Wednesday afternoon, though not necessarily at the resorts. Restaurants in the cities are often closed on Sunday.

Banking hours vary between branches and regions. Most are open from 8am to 1pm, though some reopen after lunch until 3pm. Some banks stay open until 4:30pm on Friday.

Accommodations

Accommodations in Belize range from exclusive resorts to charming bed-and-breakfasts, basic dive lodges, backpacker hostels and tents on the beach. Concentrated along the coast and offshore cayes, most resorts cater to watersports enthusiasts and, of course, divers. Ambergris Caye has the most to offer, though Caye Caulker and Placencia are gaining ground and offer cheaper accommodations and services.

The outer cayes and atolls offer both full-service resorts and rustic lodgings, and most provide all the basic amenities, though you should expect less in the way of facilities and activities. Belize City options range from small guesthouses

Slickrock Adventures' lodgings on Glover's Reef are typical of many rustic offshore resorts.

and hotels to international chain hotels. See Listings (pages 128-132) for contact information.

Belize's 7% value-added tax applies to all hotel expenses. If you stay in a small hotel or guesthouse just one night and don't insist on a receipt, you may not be charged the tax.

Dining & Food

Restaurant menus in Belize borrow largely from international cuisine. Resort cuisine, in particular, is directed toward U.S. and Mexican tastes. Expect everything from burgers to tacos, often with a local side dish such as rice and beans or fried plantain, which tastes like sweet potato chips. Popular with locals and tourists alike, fresh seafood is available at almost every hotel and restaurant. To find regional cuisine, you'll have to travel inland.

Food on live-aboard boats usually features U.S. and Caribbean cuisine. Endless snacks and substantial portions will give you the energy for four or five dives a day.

Street vendors in Belize City and the larger towns sell fruit, sandwiches, snacks and nuts. Look for signs of poor hygiene to avoid stomach woes.

What About the Water?

Although water is plentiful on the mainland, the offshore cayes rely mostly on natural aquifers to provide their freshwater needs. Despite high annual rainfall, the demand on larger resort islands often outstrips the supply from groundwater reservoirs. Many turn to desalinated water. On smaller islands you may be asked to help save water by showering only once a day.

Because the natural supplies are often brackish, it's not advisable to drink tap water. Bottled water is widely available. Use it for drinking and brushing your teeth — many larger hotels provide guests with daily pitchers of bottled water. Even when traveling on the mainland, drink only bottled water to ensure you remain healthy throughout your trip.

Shopping

Belize City, Ambergris Caye and Placencia offer a wide array of souvenir shops that sell everything from T-shirts to local crafts, which include ceramics, paintings and jewelry. Dangriga also has a good range of stores and shops. Shopping options are predictably limited on the smaller cayes and atolls. Stores stock the basics, but many items have to be ordered and shipped from the mainland.

Avoid purchasing items made from coral, black coral, turtle shells or seashells. While you may find these items for sale, harvesting them is largely illegal, and importing them into your home country is likely forbidden under international treaty.

Activities & Attractions

Belize has much to offer in addition to excellent diving, including virgin rainforests, exotic wildlife, ancient Mayan ruins, hiking and a host of other adventurous activities. If you or a nondiving partner seek additional distractions, need a break from diving or simply want to visit the mainland, following are a few suggestions to help you plan.

ANDREW MARSHALL AND LEANNE WALKER

Belize Zoo

About 30 miles (48km) west of Belize City off the Western Highway, the Belize Zoo (☎ 820-2004, www.belizezoo.org) traces its origins to the wildlife film industry. It was founded in 1983 following production of *Path of the Rain Gods*, when a trainer realized that many of the film's formerly wild stars were now in fact tame and would not survive without help. The zoo has since expanded into a successful wildlife and tropical education center.

More than 125 animals are kept in natural habitats that extend over 29 acres (12 hectares). Most of Belize's indigenous species are represented, including Baird's tapir (the national animal), jaguars, howler monkeys, crocodiles and a variety of tropical birds. These animals were either orphaned, rehabilitated, born at the zoo or received as gifts from other zoological institutions. Efforts are made to release many of them back into the wild.

TOM BOYDEN

Found both in captivity and in the wild, the endangered Baird's tapir is Belize's national animal.

23

Crooked Tree Wildlife Sanctuary

This wildlife sanctuary protects 5 sq miles (8 sq km) around the village of Crooked Tree, 33 miles (53km) northwest of Belize City. During the dry season (November to May) the area's rivers, swamps and lagoons attract flocks of migrating birds. Birdwatchers have spotted some 275 species, including ducks, herons, kites, egrets, kingfishers, ospreys and hawks. One notable visitor is the jabiru stork, the largest flying bird in the Western Hemisphere. Boasting wing-spans of more than 10ft (3m), the storks nest in the lowland pine savannas. Other sanctuary residents include black howler monkeys, coatis, Morelet's crocodiles, iguanas and turtles.

Tours usually include a boat trip through the lagoon, a walk along the elevated boardwalk and viewing time atop the observation towers. For more information contact the Belize Audubon Society (☎ 223-5004, www.belize audubon.org).

CAROLYN MILLER

Vistors to Crooked Tree can roam the boardwalk to spot resident wildlife.

Bermudian Landing Community Baboon Sanctuary

Troops of endangered black howler monkeys spend their days foraging in the treetops.

Baboon is actually the local name for the black howler monkey, an endangered species that exists only in Belize. Established in 1985 with help from local farmers, the sanctuary protects a stretch of forest along the banks of the Belize River, the animal's natural habitat. If you want to hear the monkeys' unmistakable howls, plan to visit the sanctuary at dawn or dusk, though the troops are approachable throughout the day.

A guide is mandatory, as all land in the sanctuary is privately owned. Several agencies offer tours, or you can make arrangements at the sanctuary visitors center (☎ 220-2181) in the village of Bermudian Landing. For more information email the sanctuary at baboon@btl.net.

Guanacaste National Park

One of Belize's smaller reserves, Guanacaste National Park covers some 50 acres (20 hectares). The park is named after a giant guanacaste tree a short

GREG JOHNSTON

Guanacaste supports a wealth of tropical flora.

walk from the park entrance. This prized hardwood tree survived the ravages of time and woodcutters' axes to rise high above the jungle floor. You'll find dozens of other lush tropical plant species, including spectacular wild orchids, as well as many native birds and mammals.

Guanacaste lies just 2.5 miles (4km) east of the capital, Belmopan. Open daily, the visitors center provides brochures about the park's 2 miles (3km) of self-guided trails. For more information contact the Belize Audubon Society (☎ 223-5004, www.belizeaudubon.org).

Gales Point Wildlife Sanctuary

Some 25 miles south of Belize City, the Creole village of Gales Point sits at the tip of a narrow peninsula on the south end of Southern Lagoon. Fed by the Manatee River, the lagoon has long been a favorite gathering spot for large numbers of endangered American manatees. A distant cousin of the elephant, these lumbering marine herbivores reach 13ft (4m) long and weigh up to 800 pounds (360kg). At least 70 manatees are thought to frequent the lagoon. The sanctuary protects nearly 10,000 acres (4,000 hectares) of manatee habitat and includes one of the largest turtle-nesting sites in Belize.

Local guides are available out of Gales Point. Seeing the manatees up close takes patience and luck, although several of them are fitted with radio transmitters, so guides can track their movements. Regular water taxis link Belize City and the village, which is also worth a look.

Cockscomb Basin Wildlife Sanctuary

Cockscomb Basin Wildlife Sanctuary was established in 1984 to protect the native jaguar population. Rising from 300ft (90m) above sea level to the summit of Victoria Peak at 3,675ft (1,120m), the basin shelters several wild cat species, including jaguars, jaguarundis, pumas, ocelots and margays. The lush tropical forest is also home to anteaters, armadillos, Baird's tapirs, brocket deer, kinkajous, otters, boa constrictors, 300 species of birds and myriad plant species.

The sanctuary is sprawled across more than 100,000 acres (40,000 hectares) south of Dangriga, just outside the village of Maya Centre. You can arrange a tour through a travel agency or join a guided tour from the sanctuary visitors center. Contact the Belize Audubon Society (☎ 223-5004, www.belizeaudubon.org) for more information.

A powerful symbol in ancient Mayan ritual, the jaguar still roams the wilds in Cockscomb Basin.

Mayan Ruins

Mayan civilization dominated Belize for some 3,500 years before the arrival of Spanish conquistadors in the 16th century. But the Maya's complex religious and social structure had already disintegrated, leaving only their many ruined temples and palaces. Extensive ruins lie scattered throughout Belize, though only a small number have been excavated and opened to tourists. If you find time to visit, the following Mayan ruins offer a fascinating contrast to the marine world.

Altun Ha (Rockstone Pond)

Altun Ha is one of Belize's best-known and most extensively excavated Mayan ruins. It's here that archaeologists discovered a large carved jade head depicting Kinich Ahau, the Mayan sun god. The piece has become a national symbol of Belize and appears on every Belizean banknote. The site comprises two large plazas surrounded by 13 primary temples and residential structures. Altun Ha was a major ceremonial center in the Classic period of Mayan rule (AD 250 to 900) and also served as an important trading hub, linking merchants on the Caribbean coast with Mayan cities farther inland.

The ruins are 34 miles (55km) north of Belize City, near the village of Rockstone Pond. While there's no public transportation to the ruins, many organized tours visit the site.

Lamanai (Submerged Crocodile)

One of the Maya's most important ceremonial centers, Lamanai was continuously occupied from as early as 1500 BC right through the 17th century. Though largely unexcavated, this archaeological reserve also contains a small museum and the ruins of two 16th century Spanish churches and a 19th century British sugar mill. You'll find a wealth of native plant and animal life in the surrounding tropical rainforest, including a troop of howler monkeys.

Lamanai sits on the banks of the New River Lagoon in north central Belize and is readily accessible by road or the river itself, perhaps the most stunning way to approach it. (Protect yourself from the sun, and look for crocodiles along the riverbanks.) The site is well developed for tourism, with a variety of nearby accommodations.

Xunantunich (Stone Maiden)

One of the smaller Mayan sites, Xunantunich (pronounced soo-NAHN-too-neech) was a major ceremonial center during the Classic period. Substantial

KEVIN MCDONNELL
Restored carvings grace the towering facade of El Castillo, Xunantunich's main temple.

excavation has unearthed three plazas surrounded by more than two dozen temples and palaces. The central temple, El Castillo (The Castle), rises 130ft (40m) and offers stunning views of the Maya Mountains and neighboring Guatemala. Excavations are ongoing—visit the small visitors center for updates on current findings.

Xunantunich overlooks the Mopán River opposite the village of San José Succotz, 8 miles (13km) southwest of San Ignacio. This is one of the most accessible sites via public transportation or a tour group. From San José Succotz you'll cross the river on a small ferry and either walk or ride uphill a mile to the ruins.

Caracol

The largest known Mayan ruins in Belize, Caracol was rediscovered in the 1930s, though it wasn't until 1950 that excavation began. A regional power during the Classic period, Caracol takes its name from the Spanish word for snail. The site's highest pyramid, Caana (Sky Palace), rises 140ft (43m) and was until recent years the tallest manmade structure in Belize. The ruins are still under excavation, and while there you may witness the archaeological dig in progress.

Near the Guatemalan border, about 50 miles (80km) south of San Ignacio, Caracol is one of the more inaccessible sites in Belize. Other than a small visitors center, there are no services, and roads are impassable during the rainy season. Construction of a new access road was slated to begin in 2002, but it's best to have a reputable tour operator arrange your visit. If you plan to drive to the site yourself, contact the Belize Department of Archaeology in Belmopan (☎ 822-2106) or the Forestry Department in Douglas da Silva to check current road conditions.

Lubaantun (Fallen Stones)

An important ceremonial center, Lubaantun flourished in the Late Classic period (AD 600 to 900). The partially excavated ruins comprise 11 primary structures grouped around five main plazas and three ball courts. The construction style is unique, as structures are built entirely of carefully fitted, hand-cut limestone blocks assembled without mortar.

The ruins are perched atop an isolated ridge near the village of San Pedro Columbia, about 25 miles (40km) northwest of Punta Gorda. Public transportation to the site is unreliable, so you should arrange a visit with a tour operator out of Punta Gorda. Include stops at nearby traditional Maya villages for a glimpse of Belize's indigenous culture.

Diving Health & Safety

Belize is a safe destination and poses few health risks to visitors. Your greatest concern should be the tropical sun. Keep to the shade whenever possible and drink more water than you normally might to avoid dehydration, which can increase your risk of decompression sickness. Use waterproof sunblock with a high sun protection factor (at least SPF 30), and reapply it frequently, especially after being in the water. Also wear protective clothing, including sunglasses and a wide-brimmed hat.

Watch what you eat and drink. Make sure food is both fresh and well cooked, particularly shellfish—conch and lobster spoil very quickly in the tropics. Eat fruit you can peel and avoid salads, unless you're sure they've been thoroughly washed. Drink only bottled water or bottled fruit drinks and sodas.

Entry into Belize does not require mandatory vaccinations. That said, you may want to consider certain vaccinations (e.g., tetanus, typhoid, hepatitis, rabies, etc.), particularly if you plan to go inland. Some of these vaccinations are administered in two or three parts over several weeks, so plan well ahead.

There are occasional cases of mosquito-borne malaria, especially in rural areas. Consult your doctor or pharmacist well before you leave to obtain the correct prophylactic—bear in mind that some drugs (e.g., Larium) can induce unusual side effects not compatible with diving. Take the drug a few weeks before your trip to see if you have an adverse reaction. Most of all, protect yourself against being bitten by using plenty of insect repellent and wearing long pants and long-sleeved shirts in the evenings.

The U.S. Centers for Disease Control & Prevention regularly posts updates on health-related concerns around the world specifically for travelers. Contact the CDC by fax or visit their website. Call (toll-free from the U.S.) ☎ 888-232-3299 and request Document 000005 to receive a list of documents available by fax. The website is www.cdc.gov.

Diving & Flying

Most divers in Belize arrive by plane. While it's fine to dive soon *after* flying, it's important to remember that your last dive should be completed at least 24 hours *before* your flight to minimize the risk of decompression sickness, caused by residual nitrogen in the blood.

Pre-Trip Preparation

Your general state of health, diving skill level and specific equipment needs are the three most important factors that impact any dive trip. If you honestly assess these before you leave home, you'll be well on your way to assuring a safe dive trip.

Tips for Evaluating a Dive Boat

Dive boats can be anything from fragile skiffs to elegant live-aboards. Most of the dive boats you'll encounter in Belize are of sound quality and designed for the job. However, you should always take a good look at the craft you'll be diving from before you leave the dock.

A well-outfitted dive boat has a radio for communication with onshore services. It also carries oxygen, a recall device and a first-aid kit. A well-prepared crew will give a thorough predive briefing that explains procedures for dealing with an emergency when divers are in the water. The briefing will also explain how divers should enter the water and get back onboard. A larger boat should have a shaded area, a supply of fresh drinking water and a head (marine toilet).

In a strong current, the crew might provide a special descent line and should be able to throw out a drift line from the stern. On larger boats with smaller tenders, the tender should always be available to pick up a drifting diver or one who may surface with a problem. Whatever size vessel, the crew should always be alert to the possibility of a diver surfacing away from the boat and be ready to respond in an emergency.

For deep dives the crew should hang a safety tank at 15ft (5m). On night dives a good boat will have powerful lights, including a strobe light.

When dealing with groups, a good crew will get everyone's name on a dive roster so it can initiate an immediate search if a diver is missing. This is something you should always verify.

First, if you're not in shape, start exercising. Second, if you haven't dived for a while (six months is too long), and your skills are rusty, do a local dive with an experienced buddy or take a scuba review course. Feeling good physically and diving regularly will make you a safer diver and enhance your enjoyment underwater.

At least a month before your trip, inspect your dive gear. Remember, your regulator should be serviced annually, whether you've used it or not. If you use a dive computer and can replace the battery yourself, change it before the trip or buy a spare one to take along. Otherwise, send the computer to the manufacturer for a battery replacement.

If possible, find out if the dive center you'll be using rents or services the type of gear you own. If not, you might want to take spare parts or even spare gear. A spare mask is always a good idea.

Purchase any additional equipment you might need, such as a dive light and tank marker light for night diving, a line reel for wreck diving, etc. Make sure you have at least a whistle attached to your BC. Better yet, add a marker tube (also known as a safety sausage or come-to-me).

About a week before taking off, do a final check of your gear, grease o-rings, check batteries and assemble a save-a-dive kit. This kit should at minimum contain spare mask and fin straps, snorkel keeper, mouthpiece, valve cap, zip ties and o-rings. Don't forget to pack a first-aid kit and medications such as decongestants, ear drops, antihistamines and motion sickness tablets.

DAN

Divers Alert Network (DAN) is an international membership association of individuals and organizations sharing a common interest in diving and safety. It operates a 24-hour diving emergency hot line in the U.S.: ☎ **919-684-8111** or **919-684-4DAN** (-4326). The latter accepts collect calls in a dive emergency.

Though DAN does not directly provide medical care, it does offer advice on early treatment, evacuation, and hyperbaric treatment of diving-related injuries. Divers should contact DAN for assistance as soon as a diving emergency is suspected.

DAN membership is reasonably priced and includes DAN TravelAssist, a benefit that covers medical air evacuation from anywhere in the world for any illness or injury. For a small additional fee, divers can get secondary insurance coverage for decompression illness. For membership details, contact DAN at ☎ 800-446-2671 in the U.S. or ☎ 919-684-2948 elsewhere. DAN can also be reached at www.diversalertnetwork.org.

Medical & Recompression Facilities

For minor illnesses contact a doctor through your hotel or visit the Karl Heusner Memorial Hospital in Belize City. For more serious complaints consider air evacuation to Houston, Miami or New Orleans.

Subaquatics operates the only recompression facility in Belize, adjacent to the airport on Ambergris Caye. Local dive operators fund the chamber and support staff. You may be asked to donate $1 per tank dived as a contribution to their efforts.

Medical Contacts

Medical Facilities

Karl Heusner Memorial Hospital
Princess Margaret Drive
Belize City
☎ 223-1548 fax: 223-3081
www.khmh.org

San Carlos Medical Clinic,
Pharmacy & Pathology Lab
Pescador Drive
San Pedro
Ambergris Caye
☎ 226-2918

Recompression Chamber

Subaquatics of Belize
emergency ☎ 226-2851
☎ 226-3195 fax: 226-2852
sssbelize@aol.com

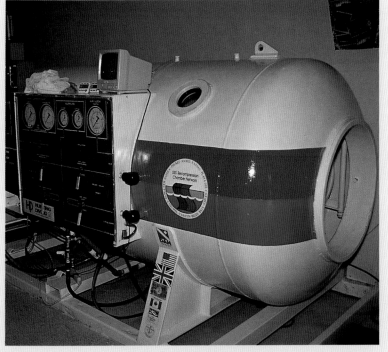

Be careful when diving remote sites, as the nearest chamber is on Ambergris Caye.

Diving in Belize

While Belize consistently ranks among the top three Caribbean dive destinations, the diving industry here has not developed at the same furious pace as at other locations, so it's still possible to find uncrowded reefs and enjoy a less commercialized setting ashore. Most dive sites lie along the barrier reef and offshore cayes and atolls and are accessed by boat, with a handful of shore dives off Tobacco Caye, South Water Caye and the atolls. This guide highlights some of the most popular sites in each region. Keep in mind that there are countless others, including those that have yet to be named or even discovered.

Underwater, the regions share many topographical similarities. Generally speaking, shallow coral gardens, sandy plains and turtle grass beds lead to complex spur-and-groove formations, which plunge over sheer walls to depth. But each region is distinguished by subtle changes in coral growth and marine life.

Most of the dive sites are ideal for repetitive diving, as many of the walls start in only 20 to 50ft (6 to 15m) and are topped by shallow sandy areas with flourishing coral formations. Most shore-based operators offer two-tank trips in the morning and afternoon, while live-aboards schedule as many as five dives a day if you have the energy.

The dive sites described in this guide are divided into four main regions, largely classified according to the point of departure. Sites in the northern cayes

World-Renowned Protection

Belize has long recognized the value of its natural assets, particularly with respect to tourism. To protect areas that are environmentally fragile or of particular interest, the country manages a national park system, which includes several of the most popular diving areas. These efforts received international recognition in October 1996, when seven of the protected areas on the reef were collectively named a World Heritage Site under UNESCO's World Heritage Convention. Known as the Belize Barrier Reef Reserve System, the site encompasses about 370 sq miles (960 sq km) and includes Bacalar Chico National Park & Marine Reserve, Blue Hole Natural Monument, Half Moon Caye Natural Monument, Glover's Reef Marine Reserve, South Water Caye Marine Reserve, Laughing Bird Caye National Park and Sapodilla Cayes Marine Reserve. Visiting divers are encouraged to follow a "look but don't touch" approach and practice good buoyancy control to avoid damaging the reef.

are accessed from Belize City, Ambergris Caye or Caye Caulker, while those in the middle cayes are accessed from Dangriga and sites in the southern cayes from Placencia. The three offshore atolls are presented as a separate region, though they can be reached from a number of locations. You can choose an extended daytrip from one of the main departure points and islands or transfer to a resort on the offshore atolls. Alternatively, you can choose one of the live-aboard boats, which generally concentrate their diving on the atolls.

Dive Training & Certification

While visiting Belize, you can try a dive to see if the sport appeals to you, enroll in a certification course or further your diving skills. Most dive centers offer courses ranging from basic Open Water through Divemaster, as well as specialty courses such as nitrox diving, deep diving, night diving, etc. One option for student divers is the referral program, in which you do the classroom work at a dive center close to home, then complete your open-water dives with a dive center in Belize.

Both live-aboard boats operating in Belize also offer a wide range of diving courses.

Check the Listings section (pages 130-132) for contact information.

Snorkeling

For many of us, snorkeling is our introduction to the wonders of the marine world. Belize is blessed with countless exceptional snorkeling sites, particularly along the patch and fringing reefs that surround the cayes and atolls. Most lie within the barrier reef or atoll lagoons, protected from ocean swells and strong currents.

Many dive operators and resorts offer trips for both novice and experienced snorkelers. These excursions often venture to remote shallow reefs, where you'll find myriad reef fish and may spot rays, nurse sharks or even the occasional manatee. Day boats and the larger resorts provide each guest with a mask, snorkel and fins, though experienced snorkelers may want to bring their own familiar gear.

Beware the risk of sunburn while snorkeling, as the cool water can mask the sun's effects until it's too late. Wear a good waterproof sunblock and a T-shirt or lycra dive skin for extra protection.

Live-Aboards

For the dedicated diver and photographer a live-aboard trip is perhaps the best option. Live-aboards range much farther than day boats during a one-week charter and often visit seldom-dived or even newly discovered sites.

Belize's Top Snorkeling Spots

Northern Cayes

Ambergris Caye
Hol Chan Cut
Shark-Ray Alley
Mexico Rocks

Caye Caulker
Stingray Village
The Split

Middle Cayes

South Water Caye
Tobacco Caye

Southern Cayes

Laughing Bird Caye
Silk (Queen) Cayes
Pompion Caye
Mosquito Caye
Scipio Cayes
Colson Cayes
Bird Cayes

Offshore Atolls

Turneffe Islands
Blue Creek
Hollywood

Lighthouse Reef
Eagle Ray Wall
Half Moon Flats
Sand Bore

Glover's Reef
Long Caye
Emerald Forest

ANDREW MARSHALL AND LEANNE WALKER

There's the added benefit of not having to lug your equipment bag to the boat each morning.

Two live-aboards operate in Belizean waters (see Listings, page 132), both aimed at the luxury end of the market. While these may seem expensive at first glance, consider the per-dive cost (particularly if you want to dive the atolls) and the fact that your accommodation, meals and drinks are included.

However, no matter how comfortable, life at sea is not for everyone. If you must feel the sand between your toes or indulge in the evening distractions only a resort can provide, then a live-aboard is probably not for you.

Day Boats

A variety of day boats operate among the cayes, ranging from simple skiffs to large powerboats with all the amenities. Most are locally built and piloted by experienced local captains. The smaller boats are used for fast trips to the reef, while the larger boats offer comfortable passage to the offshore reefs and atolls. Although most day boats have some sort of awning over at least part of the deck, bring a wide-brimmed hat and plenty of sunblock to protect yourself before and after each dive.

Day boats include fast powerboats, built to whisk divers to sites along the offshore cayes.

Dive Site Icons

The symbols at the beginning of each dive site description provide a quick summary of some of the following characteristics present at each site:

 Good snorkeling or free-diving site.

 Remains or partial remains of a wreck can be seen at this site.

 Sheer wall or drop-off.

 Deep dive. Features of this dive occur in water deeper than 90ft (27m).

 Strong currents may be encountered at this site.

 Strong surge (the horizontal movement of water caused by waves) may be encountered at this site.

 Drift dive. Because of strong currents and/or difficulty in anchoring, a drift dive is recommended at this site.

 Beach/shore dive. This site can be accessed from shore.

 Poor visibility. The site often has visibility of less than 40ft (12m).

 Caves are a prominent feature of this site. Only experienced cave divers should explore inner cave areas.

 Marine preserve. Special regulations apply in this area.

 Decompression dive. This site reaches depths that require single or multiple safety decompression stops.

Pisces Rating System for Dives & Divers

The dive sites in this book are rated according to the following diver skill-level rating system. These are not absolute ratings but apply to divers at a particular time, diving at a particular place. For instance, someone unfamiliar with prevailing conditions might be considered a novice diver at one dive area, but an intermediate diver at another, more familiar location.

Novice: A novice diver should be accompanied by an instructor, divemaster or advanced diver on all dives. A novice diver generally fits the following profile:
◆ basic scuba certification from an internationally recognized certifying agency
◆ dives infrequently (less than one trip a year)
◆ logged fewer than 25 total dives
◆ little or no experience diving in similar waters and conditions
◆ dives no deeper than 60ft (18m)

Intermediate: An intermediate diver generally fits the following profile:
◆ may have participated in some form of continuing diver education
◆ logged between 25 and 100 dives
◆ dives no deeper than 130ft (40m)
◆ has been diving in similar waters and conditions within the last six months

Advanced: An advanced diver generally fits the following profile:
◆ advanced certification
◆ has been diving for more than two years and logged over 100 dives
◆ has been diving in similar waters and conditions within the last six months

Regardless of your skill level, you should be in good physical condition and know your limitations. If you are uncertain of your own level of expertise for a particular site, ask the advice of a local dive instructor. He or she is best qualified to assess your abilities based on the site's prevailing dive conditions. Ultimately, however, you must decide if you are capable of making a particular dive, a decision that should take into account your level of training, recent experience and physical condition, as well as the conditions at the site. Remember that conditions can change at any time, even during a dive.

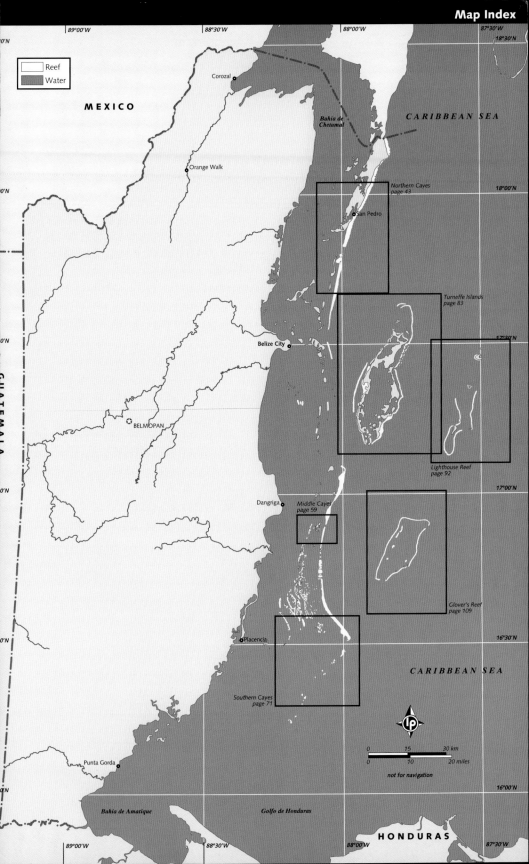

Reef
Water

MEXICO

Corozal

Bahía de Chetumal

CARIBBEAN SEA

Orange Walk

Northern Cayes page 43

San Pedro

Turneffe Islands page 83

Belize City

✪ BELMOPAN

Lighthouse Reef page 92

GUATEMALA

Dangriga

Middle Cayes page 59

Glover's Reef page 109

Placencia

Southern Cayes page 71

CARIBBEAN SEA

0   15   30 km
0   10   20 miles

not for navigation

Punta Gorda

Bahía de Amatique   *Golfo de Honduras*

HONDURAS

Northern Cayes Dive Sites

Ambergris Caye and Caye Caulker are the most popular tourist destinations along the northern stretch of the barrier reef. The cayes' dive operators visit many of the same sites along the barrier reef and offer trips to the offshore atolls. The Turneffe Islands are about an hour by boat, while the trip to Lighthouse Reef runs two hours or more, depending on sea conditions. These rides can be arduous if the weather turns rough. Some dive centers offer two-day excursions to Lighthouse Reef, which includes overnight camping on Half Moon Caye. You can also arrange daytrips to the barrier reef and atolls from Belize City, home to two major dive operators.

The largest and most developed offshore island, Ambergris Caye sits just 1 mile (1.6km) inside the barrier reef, which parallels the island shoreline for 25 miles (40km). The caye is a quick plane or boat ride from Belize City, which is 36 miles

Northern Cayes Dive Sites	Good Snorkeling	Novice	Intermediate	Advanced
1 Mexico Rocks	●	●		
2 Statue			●	
3 Tres Cocos			●	
4 Tackle Box Canyons			●	
5 Mermaids' Lair			●	
6 Esmarelda		●		
7 Boca Ciega			●	
8 Cypress Tunnels			●	
9 Pillar Coral		●		
10 Hol Chan Cut	●	●		
11 Shark-Ray Alley	●	●		
12 Amigos' Wreck			●	
13 Coral Canyons			●	
14 Stingray Village	●	●		
15 Caye Chapel Reef			●	

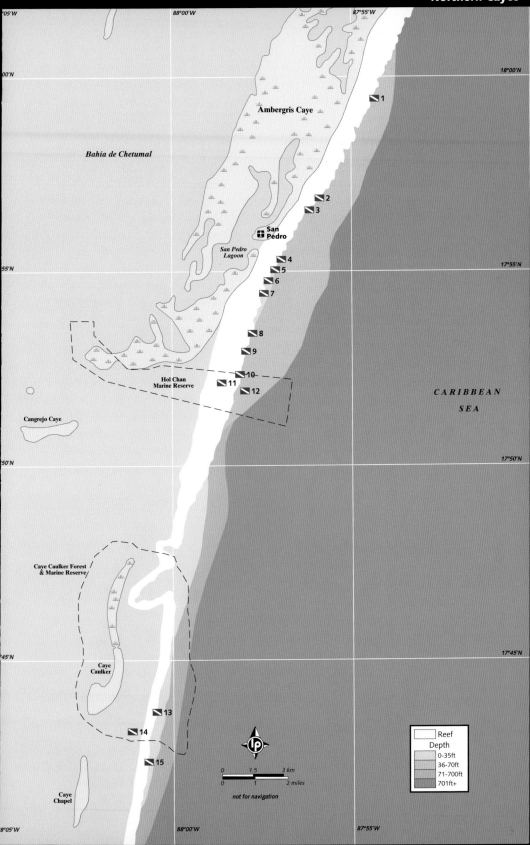

Northern Cayes

87°05'W · 88°00'W · 87°55'W

18°00'N

Ambergris Caye

Bahía de Chetumal

☒ 1

☒ 2
☒ 3

San Pedro

San Pedro Lagoon

17°55'N

☒ 4
☒ 5
☒ 6
☒ 7

☒ 8

☒ 9

☒ 10
Hol Chan Marine Reserve ☒ 11
☒ 12

CARIBBEAN SEA

Cangrejo Caye

17°50'N

Caye Caulker Forest & Marine Reserve

17°45'N

Caye Caulker

☒ 13

☒ 14

☒ 15

Caye Chapel

| | Reef |
| Depth |
| 0-35ft |
| 36-70ft |
| 71-700ft |
| 701ft+ |

0   1.5   3 km
0   1   2 miles

not for navigation

88°05'W · 88°00'W · 87°55'W

(58km) southwest. The proximity of the reef means dive operators can choose from a variety of sites and avoid overcrowding. Off the south shore is the Hol Chan Marine Reserve, where snorkelers and divers alike enjoy shallow waters and abundant marine life.

The hub of activity is the town of San Pedro, on the island's south end. This former fishing village has evolved into a world-class diving center. Although densely developed in places, the town remains unmarred by high-rise developments. San Pedro hums gently rather than buzzes, with plenty of après-dive activities, including several annual fiestas, numerous beach parties, two discos and many bars and restaurants. There are only three main streets, so you're never more than a short walk from shore and the dive centers. Most accommodations overlook the boat docks and jetties.

Some 10 miles (16km) south is Caye Caulker, a popular choice among budget travelers, as it's less developed than Ambergris Caye. This compact island is only 5 miles (8km) long and at most a half mile (.8km) wide. Most visitors arrive from Belize City, 21 miles (34km) southwest. The trip takes 45 minutes by water taxi, or you can choose to fly, a much quicker but more expensive option. One romantic notion holds that the caye's name derives from pirates who caulked their boats on the island's beaches, although it's more likely a mispronunciation of the original Spanish name, *Cayo Hicaco* (Coco Plum Caye), after the fruit trees that grow here in abundance.

The sole village is on the south end of the island, while the north end is swampy and dominated by mangroves. The ends are divided by a shallow waterway known locally as The Split, which was carved by Hurricane Hattie in 1961. The pace of life here is most definitely Caribbean, even more laid-back than on

Life on Ambergris Caye largely centers around the San Pedro docks and beachfront.

Ambergris Caye. Still, there are a wide variety of accommodations, mostly in small hotels, guesthouses, cabanas and hostels, many built in the traditional colorful clapboard style. The barrier reef is only five minutes from the docks, and the Hol Chan Marine Reserve is a short hop north, so there are plenty of dive sites from which to choose.

This section of the barrier reef boasts spur-and-groove formations, some quite massive. There are no true walls, but these formations fall quickly to deep water, and there's often a mini wall at the end of each spur.

1 Mexico Rocks

About 20 minutes or so by boat from San Pedro, this site is named after the now-defunct Mexico Cocal coconut plantation onshore. Its shallow waters and protected position inside the reef make this a perfect spot for underwater photographers, novice divers and adventurous snorkelers.

Location: 6 miles (9.7km) NE of San Pedro

Depth Range: 10-25ft (3-8m)

Access: Boat

Expertise Rating: Novice

Rising from the seafloor are numerous coral heads, some quite large. You'll find mostly brain and boulder corals decorated with purple sea fans and other branching gorgonians. The coral heads are interspersed with broad sand patches and scattered areas of seaweed and turtle grass, ideal habitat for flounder, sand divers, hermit crabs, southern stingrays and elusive batfish. Small schools of bluestriped grunts mill about the gorgonians alongside trumpetfish, which mirror the movements of the sea rods in the gentle swells. Butterflyfish, rock beauties and small wrasses are also common, and it's worth searching the reef fissures for fileclams, feather duster worms, banded coral shrimp and cleaner gobies.

When hunting, trumpetfish blend in amid sea rods.

2 | Statue

Several well-known dive destinations boast an underwater statue of Christ, perhaps to remind us that coral reefs are heavenly creations. This site is home to just such an icon. You'll probably need your divemaster's guidance to find the statue, but don't fret if you miss it, as it's really not the high point of the dive.

Location: 2 miles (3.2km) NE of San Pedro

Depth Range: 35-130ft (11-40m)

Access: Boat

Expertise Rating: Intermediate

A statue of Christ welcomes divers with open arms.

The spur-and-groove formations at this site are deep and pronounced, creating narrow canyons that are a thrill to explore in good visibility. While coral at neighboring sites has suffered some hurricane damage, particularly atop the spurs, the coral here remains healthy. Delicate staghorn and plate corals decorate the shallows, while the spurs' almost sheer sides sport numerous colorful tube sponges and small barrel sponges. Remember to glance down as you cross from one spur to the next, as the sand grooves are a favorite resting place for nurse sharks and enormous roughtail stingrays.

Usually left till the end of the dive, the statue of Christ stands atop the reef in 60ft of water. Pause for a photo, then ascend to your safety stop, where you'll be met by legions of inquisitive yellowtail snappers.

3 Tres Cocos

A few minutes northeast by boat from San Pedro, this site offers spectacular diving for those wanting to venture a little deeper. The mooring sits on the reeftop in 50ft. Covered in healthy hard corals and gorgonians, the tops of the spurs slope to about 80 or 90ft. The sand-filled grooves drop far more dramatically, bottoming out between 110 and 120ft. Watch your gauges as you follow these seaward through narrow gorges that threaten to meet overhead in places.

Location: 2 miles (3.2km) NE of San Pedro

Depth Range: 50-130ft (15-40m)

Access: Boat

Expertise Rating: Intermediate

When the visibility is good, the grooves promise fantastic wide-angle photo opportunities. Plan to take your pictures in the morning, though, as the scene turns gloomy soon after midday. For diver shots, have your buddy carry a dive light to evoke a sense of exploration and highlight sponge growth on the walls.

Rounding the ends of the spurs, look seaward to spot shoals of Atlantic spadefish, dog snappers, horse-eye jacks and, if you're lucky, the occasional reef shark. You'll find all the usual reef fish species amid the coral growth atop the spurs. As you make your way back to the shallows, swim across one or two of the grooves, looking down into their narrow, twisting depths.

The deep sand grooves here are quite dramatic.

4 Tackle Box Canyons

Directly offshore from a popular beach-side bar once named the Tackle Box, this site offers a dramatic take on the region's typical spur-and-groove reef structure. Extending seaward from the mooring, many of the gullies are deep and narrow, with near-vertical walls. You'll also find numerous swim-throughs and tunnels, all relatively short and navigable without a dive light. Marine life in these formations is generally sparse, although you're likely to encounter large lobsters and perhaps a sleeping nurse shark.

The reeftop supports abundant coral, sponge and gorgonian growth. Resident fish life ranges from the tiniest tropicals

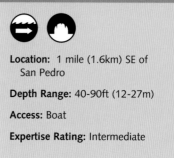

Location: 1 mile (1.6km) SE of San Pedro

Depth Range: 40-90ft (12-27m)

Access: Boat

Expertise Rating: Intermediate

to larger species like moray eels. Look closely among the corals, sponges and algae for members of the macro community, including various blennies, nudibranchs and shrimp, as well as tube worms and vivid golden crinoids.

Holed up inside a sponge, this golden crinoid reaches its feathery arms into the current to feed.

5 Mermaids' Lair

Sorry, you won't meet any mermaids, but you will find many other marine species at this attractive reef just a few minutes from San Pedro. Although the dive is rated intermediate due to the maximum depth, it's really suitable for divers of all experience levels when accompanied by a divemaster. Bring your camera for a chance at some great fish portraits, particularly if you have the patience to stay in one spot for a while.

Location: 1 mile (1.6km) SE of San Pedro

Depth Range: 40-100ft (12-30m)

Access: Boat

Expertise Rating: Intermediate

Carefully search the shallow garden of tall gorgonians to find slender filefish, sharpnose puffers and trumpetfish, all of which hide amid the swaying branches. Farther seaward the gorgonians give way to hard corals, featuring impressive stands of lettuce, boulder, brain, star and staghorn corals. You can follow the gullies to the deep reef, though it's often more rewarding to pause and observe life amid this coral metropolis. Pairs of French and gray angelfish promenade regally over the reef, parrotfish chew furiously at the coral and crowds of bluestriped grunts hover in place, almost daring you to come closer. This busy site is also a good place to look for such odd-looking species as scrawled filefish,

angular cowfish and small trunkfish, which maneuver gracefully over the reef to peck at morsels with little trumpet-shaped mouths.

You'll recognize the honeycomb cowfish by its tiny "horns."

6 Esmarelda

Just offshore from San Pedro, outside shallow Tuffy Cut, Esmarelda is often done as a second dive, as the spur-and-groove formations here are a bit less deep than at neighboring sites. Regular currents usually mean clear visibility through late afternoon, though conditions are best in the morning if you're planning wide-angle photography.

Location: 1.5 miles (2.4km) SE of San Pedro

Depth Range: 30-60ft (9-18m)

Access: Boat

Expertise Rating: Novice

From the mooring follow the spurs or gullies seaward. You'll find lots of staghorn, elkhorn, brain and lettuce corals amid lush gorgonians. There's no substantial sponge growth until you get a little deeper, but there are many small vibrant azure vase sponges, which are often home to alien-looking arrow crabs.

There's plenty of fish life on the reeftop, notably squirrelfish, schoolmasters and shoals of blue tangs. Head deeper to explore numerous narrow swim-throughs, and watch the blue water for pairs of spotted eagle rays and large pelagics.

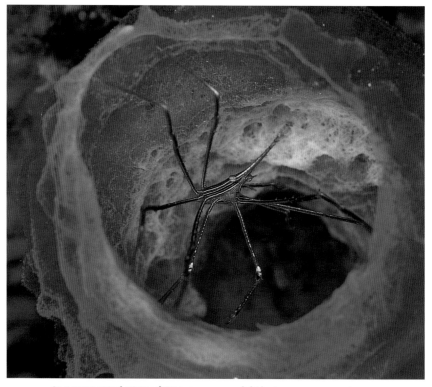

In a scene out of science fiction, an arrow crab hides in an azure vase sponge.

7 Boca Ciega

Not to be confused with a sinkhole of the same name in Hol Chan Marine Reserve, Boca Ciega is one of several sites within 10 minutes of the San Pedro docks. This reef features the familiar spur-and-groove formations, though the grooves here are somewhat broader than at adjacent sites, and the sand chutes drop quickly to depths below 100ft. The mooring is in 45ft amid lush purple sea fans and other branching gorgonians. A pair of large resident black groupers may greet you on your descent and shadow you throughout the dive.

Head deep first to look for resting nurse sharks and the occasional curious Caribbean reef shark, which patrol the depths beyond the spurs. When you reach your max depth or the end of a sand chute, cross to an adjacent groove and meander back to the mooring. Search the many overhangs and caves to find lobsters, as well as green and spotted moray eels.

Location: 2 miles (3.2km) south of San Pedro

Depth Range: 45-100ft (14-30m)

Access: Boat

Expertise Rating: Intermediate

Atop the spurs, hard corals and gorgonians are interspersed with vibrant yellow tube and azure vase sponges. Among these are parrotfish, small groups of blue chromis, creole wrasses, several species of angelfish and persistent yellowtail snappers (referred to locally as Caribbean piranha). The site boasts both wide-angle and macro subjects, although you should plan your wide-angle shots for the morning or first dive of the afternoon, as light levels in the grooves fall quickly later in the day.

8 Cypress Tunnels

Divers visit this spur-and-groove reef near San Pedro to explore a series of swim-throughs and particularly long tunnels. The grooves plunge below 100ft, so check your depth regularly, especially when exiting the tunnels. Good buoyancy control is essential to avoid kicking up sand and spoiling the visibility for fellow divers. Your dive operator may insist on guiding your group through a few of the longer passages, though experienced divers may be allowed split off as a buddy pair. You'll encounter thick shoals of silversides in some tunnels. Bring a dive light

Location: 3 miles (4.8km) south of San Pedro

Depth Range: 50-100ft (15-30m)

Access: Boat

Expertise Rating: Intermediate

to appreciate the marine life and help you navigate.

When you've finished touring the tunnels, either follow one of the grooves up toward the mooring or pick a spur and check out the abundant plate, lettuce, staghorn and boulder corals. Look amid the corals for feather stars and a host of smaller fish, including triplefin and sailfin blennies, juvenile hogfish and rock beauties. Macro-photographers will find plenty of subjects in the shallows.

A sponge is a veritable mountain to this tiny triplefin, which is only an inch (2.5cm) long.

9 | Pillar Coral

This spur-and-groove reef is an annex of the Hol Chan Marine Reserve. You'll likely dive here in conjunction with a visit to nearby Hol Chan Cut and thus pay only one entry fee for both dives.

Don't be discouraged by the patches of storm-damaged staghorn coral near the mooring—as you progress seaward the spurs become well defined and the condition of the corals improves markedly. You'll find the namesake stands of healthy pillar coral along the tops of the spurs. Small schools of bluestriped grunts, schoolmasters and squirrelfish keep to the shadows between the pillars, which are also home to dozens of cleaner gobies. Pause here to spot black groupers waiting to be groomed, as well as groups of creole

Location: 3.5 miles (5.6km) south of San Pedro

Depth Range: 40-70ft (12-21m)

Access: Boat

Expertise Rating: Novice

wrasses, which hover vertically to attract the cleaners.

Around the mooring line you'll often encounter shoals of yellowtail snappers and one or two large black groupers, which despite park rules have obviously been fed and approach divers for a handout. This makes them ideal photo subjects, as they stay close and seemingly pose for the camera.

10 Hol Chan Cut

At the heart of the Hol Chan Marine Reserve, this is one of the most popular sites off Ambergris Caye and likely one of the first you'll dive, particularly if you're taking a resort course. When your boat arrives, a warden on duty near the cut will collect the daily entry fee of BZ$5 per person. Watch for boat traffic, as the moorings are usually crowded with both snorkel and dive boats.

Location: 4 miles (6.4km) south of San Pedro

Depth Range: 10-30ft (3-9m)

Access: Boat

Expertise Rating: Novice

From the moorings it's a short swim east over shallow eelgrass beds to the cut, a 30- to 45-foot-wide sandy channel flanked by a reef that rises from 30ft to just below the surface. Tidal currents often run through the channel. If the current is strong, swim to one side and make your way along the reef. If the current is gentle, cross from one side to the other as you explore.

You'll find many of the Caribbean coral species, although the hordes of visiting divers and snorkelers have done some damage. Perhaps the most striking feature is the number of fish that shoal within the cut, notably horse-eye jacks, schoolmasters and bluestriped grunts. Out in the channel you'll spot sand divers, southern stingrays and often eagle rays, while the reef walls shelter a number of green moray eels, which may leave their lairs to approach you in search of food.

When you reach the seaward end of the cut, resist the temptation to continue toward deeper water, as you might face a long, difficult swim back to the boat. Back at the mooring you'll encounter groupers and Bermuda chub, also in search of food. Photographers will have a chance at some good fish portraits.

Hol Chan Marine Reserve

Set aside in May 1987, Hol Chan Marine Reserve was the first marine reserve established in Central America. Patrolling wardens strictly enforce park rules, and each visitor must pay a BZ$5 fee toward maintenance of the park system. The reserve covers about 5 sq miles (13 sq km) and comprises three distinct habitats, which are separately zoned and clearly marked by a series of buoys.

The outermost zone encompasses the barrier reef and includes Hol Chan Cut (*hol chan* is Mayan for "small channel"). Prevailing southerly currents sweep the reef, supporting abundant coral growth and fish life, and divers can explore the area's many steep-sided swim-throughs and caves. Between the barrier reef and the southwestern tip of Ambergris Caye, the lagoon zone features seagrass beds and small coral outcrops, which support a wide range of juvenile fish species, rays and shellfish. The third zone protects the mangroves, which shelter a multitude of fish fry waiting to make the transition to the seagrass and, ultimately, the reef.

11 | Shark-Ray Alley

Local fishing boats used to clean their catch at this shallow sandy site a half mile or so from Hol Chan Cut. This activity, in turn, attracted other fish looking for an easy meal. Although fishing boats no longer stop here, dive operators continue to feed the fish, including a number of nurse sharks and southern stingrays.

Due to the heavy boat traffic and shallow water, only snorkeling is permitted. Dive boats visit the site during surface intervals. Even without scuba gear, you can get plenty close to the action—too close for some! The divemasters feed and

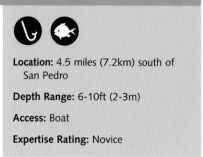

Location: 4.5 miles (7.2km) south of San Pedro

Depth Range: 6-10ft (2-3m)

Access: Boat

Expertise Rating: Novice

handle the fish, which frees you up for some great photo opportunities. While some may not approve of fish feeding, others will find this an exciting, don't-miss experience.

Feedings at Shark-Ray Alley attract dozens of nurse sharks, southern stingrays and other fish.

12 | Amigos' Wreck

This small, less-than-seaworthy interisland barge was deliberately sunk here by Amigos del Mar dive center in 1996. Though not a remarkable wreck dive, the site does offer spectacular marine life interaction, as San Pedro dive operators have established a fish-feeding station on the barge. Large nurse sharks, snappers and black groupers start to gather on the

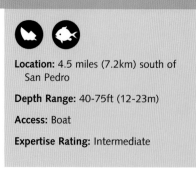

Location: 4.5 miles (7.2km) south of San Pedro

Depth Range: 40-75ft (12-23m)

Access: Boat

Expertise Rating: Intermediate

wreck as soon as a dive boat approaches. Hungry nurse sharks may even meet you at the mooring.

It's a five-minute swim seaward to the wreck site. For the best photo angles, kneel either on the sand to the starboard side of the barge or beside the divemaster atop the wreck. Sharks, groupers and large snappers crowd in close as they await their next meal. Often joining the feast is a large green moray that resides in the bow. The diners get a tad excited when dinner is served, so keep your hands to yourself, especially if you're near the divemaster. Experienced divemasters may even handle the nurse sharks, which relax into a catatonic state when gripped by the dorsal fin and flipped over. Though it remains a controversial subject among divers, fish feeding does offer an opportunity to closely approach marine life in a controlled environment.

A hungry nurse shark comes looking for a handout atop the barge.

13 Coral Canyons

One of many dive sites off Caye Caulker, Coral Canyons takes only a few minutes to reach by boat. There are few fixed moorings along this stretch of reef, so dives are made from a "live boat," which means the boatman follows the group from the surface. While locals may refer to this as a drift dive, it should not be confused with drifting in a current.

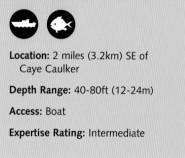

Location: 2 miles (3.2km) SE of Caye Caulker

Depth Range: 40-80ft (12-24m)

Access: Boat

Expertise Rating: Intermediate

The dive begins on a broad sandy area amid numerous small coral heads. These gradually merge into a more continuous reef structure, soon followed by the familiar spur-and-groove formation. The grooves are quite narrow and drop steeply below 100ft. Swim down into one of the grooves, searching the many overhangs and small caves for nurse sharks and roughtail stingrays. Once reaching the end of a spur, you can either cross to an adjacent groove for the return or ascend the spur and search for marine life amid the healthy hard corals and lush sponge growth.

14 Stingray Village

This shallow snorkeling site is similar to Shark-Ray Alley off Ambergris Caye. For years Caye Caulker fishermen have cleaned their sardine catch here, attracting large numbers of southern stingrays and nurse sharks. Hotels and dive centers on Cayes Caulker and Chapel now bring boatloads

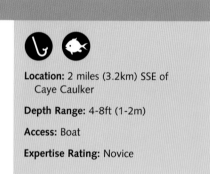

Location: 2 miles (3.2km) SSE of Caye Caulker

Depth Range: 4-8ft (1-2m)

Access: Boat

Expertise Rating: Novice

Stingrays feed on bottom-dwelling shellfish.

of snorkelers, while divers often visit during surface intervals. Whether or not your boat crew feeds them, the fish are drawn by the sound of approaching engines.

A little less busy than Shark-Ray Alley, the site allows snorkelers a close look at big fish. Photographers should use a wide-angle lens and leave their strobes on the boat (the sand reflects plenty of light). If feedings don't thrill you, you can also watch the rays and sharks feeding naturally in the sand and turtle grass.

15 Caye Chapel Reef

Caye Chapel lies some 3 miles south of Caye Caulker. While the reef here is similar to that at sites farther north, the seafloor is blanketed in silt, possibly from construction debris swept from the lagoon on the falling tide. Visibility can be particularly misty in the shallows, where swells regularly stir up the seabed.

The dive starts in 30ft among scattered low coral heads and branching gorgonians. Farther offshore the reef develops into a substantial spur-and-groove formation, with broad coral buttresses and equally wide sand chutes. Visibility also improves the deeper you go. The spurs end atop a mini wall at 70ft, which drops sharply to sand flats between 100 and 120ft, a good spot to look for large roughtail stingrays.

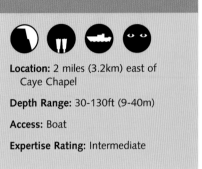

Location: 2 miles (3.2km) east of Caye Chapel

Depth Range: 30-130ft (9-40m)

Access: Boat

Expertise Rating: Intermediate

Search the reef wall and canyons to find numerous lobsters and channel clinging crabs, which normally hide during the day. Although fish are not as abundant as at other sites, macro life is impressive. Look closely amid the branching gorgonians and purple sea fans to find flamingo tongues and slender filefish. Also scour the reef for tiny secretary and arrow blennies.

Search the many reefs nooks and crevices to find Caribbean spiny lobsters.

Middle Cayes Dive Sites

At the heart of this region lies the coastal town of Dangriga, about 40 miles (64km) south of Belize City. Most visitors arrive by plane, though it's possible to drive or take a bus either from Belize City via the mostly unpaved Manatee Highway or from Belmopan via the Hummingbird Highway, a better road and quicker journey. For those seeking a mix of activities, the mainland resorts and hotels in Dangriga, Hopkins and Sittee River can arrange daytrips to sites off Tobacco and South Water Cayes and the offshore atolls. You can also arrange inland excursions to the Cockscomb Basin Wildlife Sanctuary and several Mayan ruins. If diving is your focus, Dangriga is the departure point for Tobacco Caye, South Water Caye and Glover's Reef.

Atop the barrier reef just 10 miles (16km) southeast of Dangriga is tiny 5-acre (2-hectare) Tobacco Caye, once a hideout for pirates and buccaneers. Puritans settled the caye in the mid-1600s, naming it in honor of the first tobacco crop they planted. Accommodations include several guesthouses and small hotels, which provide comfortable rooms and beach cabanas at reasonable rates. Most offer full board, as there are no restaurants on the island, though you're free to sample the fare at each hotel. Camping is also available through prior arrangement with the hotels. Nightlife is limited to a few drinks at sunset and a good book in the evening. One dive center serves guests at all the hotels. Divers can choose from many nearshore snorkeling and diving opportunities or take a daytrip to offshore Glover's Reef.

Dangriga is a sleepy town, where simply lounging in a hammock could occupy an afternoon.

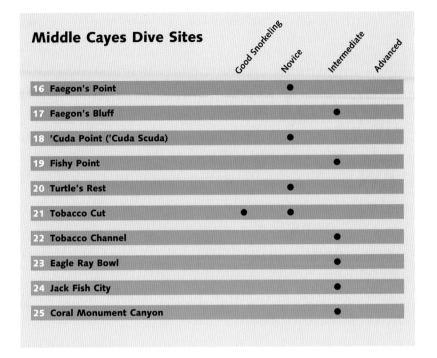

Middle Cayes Dive Sites

	Good Snorkeling	Novice	Intermediate	Advanced
16 Faegon's Point		●		
17 Faegon's Bluff			●	
18 'Cuda Point ('Cuda Scuda)		●		
19 Fishy Point			●	
20 Turtle's Rest		●		
21 Tobacco Cut	●	●		
22 Tobacco Channel			●	
23 Eagle Ray Bowl			●	
24 Jack Fish City			●	
25 Coral Monument Canyon			●	

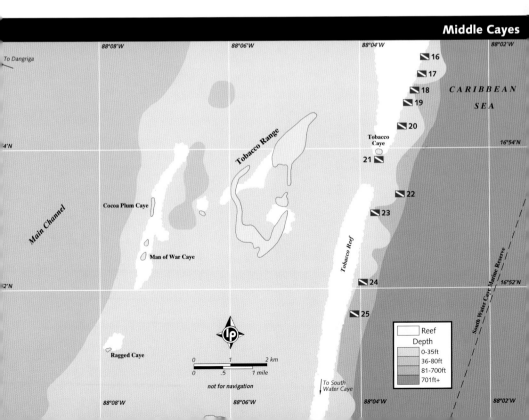

Middle Cayes

A few miles south of Tobacco Caye lies South Water Caye, a little larger at 15 acres (6 hectares). In calm conditions you can literally walk off the beach and swim to the barrier reef. The caye is at the heart of the proposed South Water Caye Marine Reserve, which will protect 62 sq miles (160 sq km) of land and water. There are two resorts on the island, both offering diving services.

As the barrier reef runs south, there is a distinct change in the reef topography. The familiar spur-and-groove formations of the north give way to what is locally known as a double-wall reef system. Broad coral buttresses slope sharply seaward from about 40ft (12m) to a wide sand channel between 100 and 120ft (30 and 37m), which is often peppered with coral outcrops and pillars. This is followed by a second reef line, which rises to about 60ft (18m) before plunging over the wall to abyssal depths. This double wall is a feature of many sites between Tobacco Reef and Gladden Spit to the south.

Despite the region's generally mild currents, many of the sites are approached as drift dives from a "live boat," which means the boatman follows divers from the surface and picks them up at a different point. This should not be confused with drift diving in a current.

16 Faegon's Point

Named for one of Tobacco Caye's resident divemasters, this is a good site for student divers, novices and those who are rusty after a long layoff from diving. Though ocean swells may stir up surge in the shal-

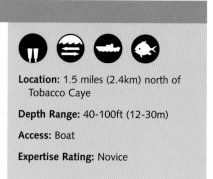

Location: 1.5 miles (2.4km) north of Tobacco Caye

Depth Range: 40-100ft (12-30m)

Access: Boat

Expertise Rating: Novice

Flamingo tongue mollusks feed on gorgonians.

lows, the entry point on open sand allows everyone to sort out their buoyancy before moving east toward a series of deep narrow grooves. Follow their twisting course past numerous low overhangs, which are favorite resting places for nurse sharks. You may only spot a shark's tail, though when discovered, they often retreat up the gully, passing inches overhead.

You can head for deeper water, but there's plenty to see between 60 and 80ft. Among the usual reef fish are boldly patterned but shy scrawled cowfish, schools of creole wrasses and juvenile hawksbill turtles, which feed on the sponges. Macrophotographers will especially appreciate the shallows, as the gorgonians are peppered with vibrant flamingo tongues, and the corals shelter banded coral shrimp, small chain morays, clusters of feather duster worms and cute secretary blennies, which peek out from tiny bore holes.

17 Faegon's Bluff

Just offshore from Tobacco Caye, this spur-and-groove reef hints at the developing double-wall reef system, with distinct reef lines divided by sandy plains. The inshore reef slopes to sand at about 120ft, though it's unnecessary to go that deep, unless you spot something worthwhile such as a cruising eagle ray. You'll find most highlights above 60ft on the gentle slope, which allows ample dive time. Overhead are shoals of needlefish and sardines, shadowed closely by prowling barracuda. Watch patiently and you may see the shoal of hunted fish turn and chase off the barracuda if it gets too close.

As on neighboring reefs, the slope here boasts lush hard corals and gorgonians. Brain and big star corals dominate, while mushroom and plate corals shelter

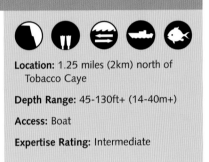

Location: 1.25 miles (2km) north of Tobacco Caye

Depth Range: 45-130ft+ (14-40m+)

Access: Boat

Expertise Rating: Intermediate

several species of juvenile reef fish. Watch for the spectacular spotted drum, in both its juvenile and intermediate stages, as well as the yellow-striped juvenile French angelfish and golden juvenile hogfish. You'll also find dozens of pairs of angelfish. Consider ascending directly from the reef, as ocean swells often stir up strong surge in the shallows.

A spotted drum doesn't develop its vivid polka dots until it reaches adulthood.

18 'Cuda Point ('Cuda Scuda)

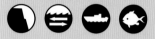

This dive starts on the inshore reef line amid narrow spurs and grooves. The sand grooves are dotted with small coral heads, while the low-profile spurs feature hard corals covered with branching gorgonians. You may face strong surge at the beginning of the dive, though its effects diminish with depth. The spurs gradually slope east to

Location: 1 mile (1.6km) north of Tobacco Caye

Depth Range: 40-80ft+ (12-24m+)

Access: Boat

Expertise Rating: Novice

Divers, especially those bearing bright objects, often stir a barracuda's curiosity.

a sandy plateau at about 80ft. You can explore this busy reef or push on to the deeper slopes.

The deeper slopes support colorful barrel, vase and tube sponges, as well as substantial growths of brain and mushroom corals. Overhangs are home to clusters of spiny lobsters, which fear-

lessly march out in plain sight of divers. The site features the whole range of Caribbean reef fish and is particularly good for photographers wanting to augment their record of species. You'll spot many bold Nassau groupers, as well as the large solitary barracuda that lend this site its name.

19 | Fishy Point

This dive begins at the base of a spur-and-groove formation on the surge-pounded barrier reef. You descend on a sandy plain at 40ft and head seaward over a wide reef slope topped by healthy thickets of branching gorgonians. Along the slope you'll find healthy sponges and corals, including many large common and deepwater sea fans, which reach into the gentle current. The largely unbroken reef drops sharply from 60ft to a deeper sandy plain at 100ft.

You could continue across the sand to the seaward slope, which ends atop a sheer wall, but this would take you below 100ft. Anyway, there's plenty of fish life to

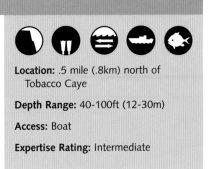

Location: .5 mile (.8km) north of Tobacco Caye

Depth Range: 40-100ft (12-30m)

Access: Boat

Expertise Rating: Intermediate

admire on the first reef slope, including large shoals of blue tangs, which rush about to forage on the algae. Check beneath overhangs to find lurking black groupers, dog snappers, French grunts and large green morays.

Blue tangs gather by the hundreds to forage along the algae-coated slope.

20 Turtle's Rest

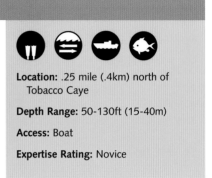

In the spring Tobacco Caye is a favored nesting area for endangered loggerhead turtles. As space is at a premium on the island, turtles even nest overnight under many of the buildings, which are raised on blocks and stilts. Before and after their nesting efforts, the turtles typically rest in reef crevices just offshore, hence the name of this site. The dive focuses on

Location: .25 mile (.4km) north of Tobacco Caye

Depth Range: 50-130ft (15-40m)

Access: Boat

Expertise Rating: Novice

The caye attracts nesting loggerhead turtles.

the inshore reef line, which comprises extensive blocks and gullies rather than the narrower spurs and grooves. Watch for surge in the shallows.

Even if you don't encounter a turtle, this site is worth exploring, as it features some fine coral and sponge growth and a diverse fish population. You're especially likely to spot juveniles of the more common reef fish. Juveniles often look completely different in their adult phase. Keep a fish ID guide handy to confirm what you've seen.

21 Tobacco Cut

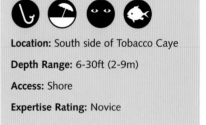

Of the few shore dives along the barrier reef, this is certainly one of the best. It's a particularly good night dive and snorkeling site. The dive starts with an easy entry beside the boat dock on the caye's southeast corner, where the reef curls around the island into the cut. A short surface swim or snorkel takes you over shallow coral outcrops to the north side of the passage. Drop down beside the sandy cut and follow the reef seaward. Stay close to the reef, as fast boats frequent the passage.

There's usually a gentle current flowing into the lagoon, which supports

Location: South side of Tobacco Caye

Depth Range: 6-30ft (2-9m)

Access: Shore

Expertise Rating: Novice

healthy coral growth and attracts a remarkable variety of fish. Watch for eagle rays (which sometimes approach the dock) and small schools of tarpon, particularly late in the day. In early spring dozens of tarpon gather in the channel to spawn.

Follow the reef out to the east face of the fringing reef, but be wary of going too far, as strong currents sometimes sweep the channel entrance, and breaking surf makes an exit there very hazardous. In the winter, occasional northerly winds drive sediment-laden water from the lagoon, dropping visibility in the cut.

Bring on the Night

If you've never been night diving, you're missing out on a magical experience. All sorts of reef creatures that hide during the day emerge at dusk, while more familiar reef fish tuck into reef nooks for the night. Photographers are able to closely approach normally skittish subjects. You'll find prowling octopuses, lobsters, mantis and red night shrimp, decorator and channel clinging crabs, feather and basket stars and a variety of nudibranchs. Use your dive light to spot resting parrotfish, butterflyfish, filefish, surgeonfish and many other species. The night hunters are also out in force, including free-swimming moray and snake eels, squirrelfish, tarpon and squid. Some fish may shadow you, waiting for you to light up an easy meal. When you return to the boat, linger awhile to watch tarpon and squid feeding on the small fish and plankton attracted by the surface lights.

Keep in mind a few basic safety precautions. It's best to dive on sites you've visited during the day, as you'll already have a feel for the terrain. A good dive light is essential, but you should also carry at least one backup light for signaling the boat in an emergency. Some boats insist on a third light source attached to your BC or tank—typically a cyalume light stick or strobe that's visible at the surface. Your boat itself should have surface lights, as well as a flashing strobe on the anchor or down line to guide you back to the boat at the end of the dive.

During the dive, keep your buddy in sight and avoid shining your light in his or her face. If you need to signal, shine the light on your hand. Be especially aware of your buoyancy to avoid damaging coral and to keep clear of the urchins that emerge at night to feed. Finally, dark water can be disorienting, so watch your gauges to monitor your bearing and ascent rate.

An octopus relies on its excellent vision when prowling the reef at night.

22 Tobacco Channel

Tobacco Cut, the reef break just south of Tobacco Caye, continues offshore as a broad sandy channel. This dive starts in 40ft of water along the first reef line, about a mile offshore from the cut. Divers head east down the slope, then hug the reef line close to the sand. You'll likely spot large nurse sharks sleeping in the sand gullies along the reef. Check the channel itself for numerous large southern and roughtail stingrays, and keep watch for pairs of passing eagle rays.

Although heavy surge has damaged coral in the shallows, the reef slope is healthy and diverse. Impressive deepwater sea fans and sponges fringe the bottom

Location: 1 mile (1.6km) SE of Tobacco Caye

Depth Range: 40-100ft (12-30m)

Access: Boat

Expertise Rating: Intermediate

of the slope, which borders a deeper sandy plain at about 100ft. You can either cross to the seaward reef line or continue to explore the first one. At the end of the dive simply follow the slope back up to your safety stop.

Stingrays often camouflage themselves beneath the sand while at rest.

23 Eagle Ray Bowl

This site marks the tail end of the spur-and-groove formations that dominate the northern section of the barrier reef. There are no fixed moorings, so the boat will follow your group as you drift dive the reef, though strong currents are rare.

The dive starts over a wide circular sandy plain, the "bowl" where eagle rays and southern stingrays commonly feed

Location: 1 mile (1.6km) south of Tobacco Caye

Depth Range: 45-100ft+ (14-30m+)

Access: Boat

Expertise Rating: Intermediate

and rest. The reef edge is split by numerous deep gullies, some of which develop into broad sand flats peppered with coral heads. As you swim east, the gentle reef slope fills in with lush hard corals and gorgonians that show little evidence of diver or hurricane damage. Fish life is also profuse, and photographers will have their pick of cooperative subjects. Among the crevices are spotted and green morays, lobsters, channel clinging crabs and banded coral shrimp.

The reef line is more pronounced as you approach the east face, which drops off below 80ft. Depending on your experience, you can plunge a little deeper or just hang on the edge awhile to watch for passing turtles and reef sharks. After a brief cruise along the wall, return to the shallows to make your ascent.

24 Jack Fish City

The double-wall reef system is more pronounced at this site. The entry point is in 50ft on a sandy plain just east of the low spur-and-groove fringing reef. You'll swim east over extensive coral buttresses, which are cut in places by sand channels. The first reef line tops out between 50 and 60ft and slopes sharply to the deeper sandy plain at 100ft. Swim across the sand to the seaward reef crest at 80ft, then plunge over the wall if your dive profile permits. It's here you'll find the drifting schools of horse-eye jacks that lend this site its name.

Return to the first reef line and explore the slope, moving north and west. As you cross the sand channels,

Location: 2 miles (3.2km) south of Tobacco Caye

Depth Range: 50-130ft (15-40m)

Access: Boat

Expertise Rating: Intermediate

look for large resting nurse sharks with accompanying remoras. You'll find deep-water sea fans and enormous barrel sponges along the upper slope. Finish your dive along the west edge of the reef amid scattered large coral heads festooned with branching gorgonians and active reef fish.

Forming vast shoals just off the wall, horse-eye jacks often closely approach divers.

25 Coral Monument Canyon

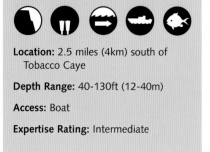

This clearly defined double-wall reef system comprises massive coral buttresses cut here and there by broad sandy canyons. The dive follows the first reef line north against the gentle current and then east onto the sandy plain that divides the double reef. In the center of this plain is a 20ft coral pillar that rises from the seabed at 115ft. You can swim by it on your way to the second reef and the wall, or descend to inspect life on this coral high-rise. The sand is home to numerous southern stingrays and

Location: 2.5 miles (4km) south of Tobacco Caye

Depth Range: 40-130ft (12-40m)

Access: Boat

Expertise Rating: Intermediate

enormous roughtail stingrays that all but ignore your approach.

If you do head for the wall, watch your depth as you shadow cubera and dog snappers and horse-eye jacks. Strong currents drive the fish into tight shoals off in the blue, where sharp eyes may also spot patrolling reef sharks. Finish your dive along the first reef slope amid shoals of grazing blue tangs. In the spring, shoals of parrotfish gather to spawn in the shallows.

This solitary coral pillar is a marine life magnet.

Southern Cayes Dive Sites

About 40 minutes flying time from Belize City, Placencia is the country's southernmost diving hub. This small town sits on the south end of a narrow 15-mile (24km) peninsula that parallels the coastline. Development here is fairly low-key. The narrow "main street" is peppered with small hotels, guesthouses, bars and restaurants that come alive in the evening. North of town, a number of full-service resorts face the seaward side of the peninsula, which locals boast offers the best beaches in Belize. You'll also find the traditional Garífuna village of Seine Bight. Like Dangriga, Placencia is an ideal base for both divers and those seeking other diversions. Inland attractions include Cockscomb Basin Wildlife Sanctuary, the Monkey River and several Mayan ruins.

The coastline south of Placencia sweeps west and diverges from the barrier reef, resulting in a much broader reef table than that to the north. Large expanses of coral reef are laced with channels that drop between 90 and 110ft (27 and 33m), then rise abruptly beside the many shoals and cayes. Sites on the barrier reef take a bit longer to reach, while those within the protection of the reef are relatively uncrowded and pristine, notably the faro reef system around Laughing Bird

Divers seek out the remote southern cayes for their powdery beaches and pristine reefs.

Think Big

While these waters do shelter a year-round population of whale sharks and manta rays, you should plan a visit south between April and June for your best chance at a sighting. Each year during this period huge shoals of cubera snappers gather to spawn in the depths off Gladden Spit. The snappers release masses of pale-colored spawn into the water column, which rises to the surface and is a positive feast for the whale sharks and mantas. Placencia dive operators discovered that divers' exhaust bubbles simulate the spawn at the surface and attract these majestic animals, which make repeated close passes while feeding.

Southern Cayes Dive Sites

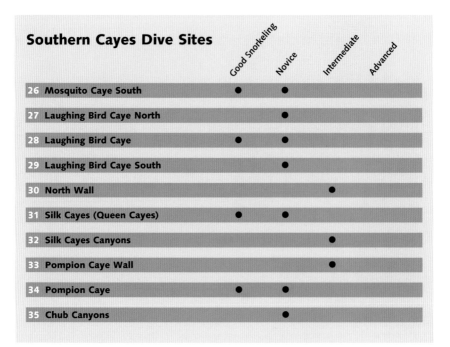

		Good Snorkeling	Novice	Intermediate	Advanced
26	Mosquito Caye South	●	●		
27	Laughing Bird Caye North		●		
28	Laughing Bird Caye	●	●		
29	Laughing Bird Caye South		●		
30	North Wall			●	
31	Silk Cayes (Queen Cayes)	●	●		
32	Silk Cayes Canyons			●	
33	Pompion Caye Wall			●	
34	Pompion Caye	●	●		
35	Chub Canyons		●		

Caye (see "Legend of the Faros," page 75). South of Gladden Spit the reef topography is a mixture of reef flats and spur-and-groove formations, both ending atop sheer walls. Divers encounter whale sharks and mantas in this region in the spring and early summer.

Dive centers in Placencia operate large, well-equipped boats with powerful twin outboards that can reach the barrier reef in about 45 minutes. The range of available sites spans from Gladden Spit up north to the Sapodilla Cayes far south. Diving highlights include spectacular drop-offs and topside intervals on any number of idyllic palm-fringed cayes.

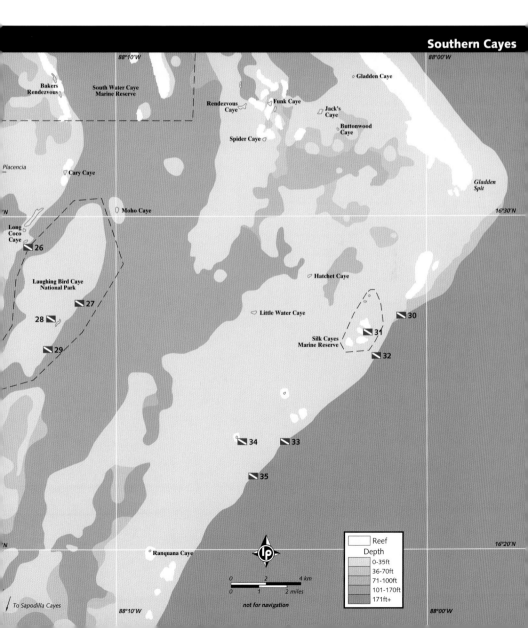

Southern Cayes

26 Mosquito Caye South

In the midst of the shallow inshore lagoon and fairly close to the mainland, this site experiences variable visibility, dependant on tides and the prevailing weather. You can snorkel or dive from the beach if your boat drops you on the caye, but be careful when roaming the shallows, as there's a healthy population of sea urchins.

Dense shoals of silversides swirl just off the beach. To find them, simply follow the pelicans and gulls that relentlessly dive-bomb the shallows to gulp down large mouthfuls of these small fish. Below the surface the baitfish race about to escape both the birds and several large tarpon. Don't be alarmed when one of these sleek predators flashes out of the murk with alarming speed.

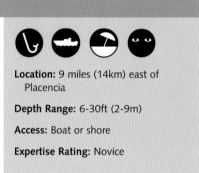

Location: 9 miles (14km) east of Placencia

Depth Range: 6-30ft (2-9m)

Access: Boat or shore

Expertise Rating: Novice

When you *are* able to glimpse the corals through the silversides, you'll spot most of the common reef fish and invertebrates. Hard corals here are in better condition than those a bit farther offshore at Laughing Bird Caye. Staghorn and stands of elkhorn coral shelter schooling grunts, angelfish, damselfish, lizardfish, hogfish and bold trumpetfish.

Safety in numbers is paramount for silversides, which are gobbled up both by birds and other fish.

27 Laughing Bird Caye North

Unlike the reef structure south of Laughing Bird Caye, the reef to the north drops off rapidly and sports denser hard-coral growth. The seabed is easily disturbed, so take time to fine-tune your buoyancy while you look for various sand-dwelling creatures such as lizardfish, batfish and pretty little yellow stingrays. Numerous upside-down

Location: .5 mile (.8km) NE of Laughing Bird Caye

Depth Range: 25-70ft (8-21m)

Access: Boat

Expertise Rating: Novice

Upside-down jellyfish "face" the sun to nourish photosynthetic algae that live within their tentacles.

jellyfish rest in the sand and mimic anemones. If disturbed, they'll gracefully rise and swim to a new location.

Ascend the hard-coral banks and search among the rope sponges for seahorses, octopuses and camouflaged frogfish, which gently wave their lures to attract small prey. Several different urchin species graze atop the reef. Also look for vivid tunicates, which often attach to rope sponges. Examine everything closely, as almost every reef cluster conceals tiny triplefin and redlip blennies, redspotted hawkfish and arrow crabs.

28 Laughing Bird Caye

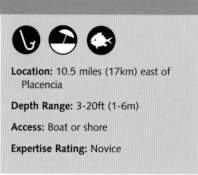

Laughing Bird Caye is named for the colonies of laughing gulls that nest here. There's a wide variety of other birdlife on the island, including brown pelicans, green herons, blackbirds, sea eagles, frigate birds and brown boobies.

Despite (and partly due to) its status as a marine reserve, the faro reef that surrounds the caye has suffered damage in recent years. Coral bleaching (thanks to El Niño), hurricane damage (from Mitch in 1998) and legions of careless daytrip snorkelers have taken their toll

Location: 10.5 miles (17km) east of Placencia

Depth Range: 3-20ft (1-6m)

Access: Boat or shore

Expertise Rating: Novice

on the nearshore corals. There are patches of healthy coral farther offshore, but few people make the effort to swim out that far. If you do, be aware of boat traffic at the surface.

At any rate, most visitors will appreciate even inshore snorkeling, as dozens of reef fish species thrive here, feeding on algae and each other. You'll likely see large barracuda and small shoals of needlefish and halfbeaks, as well as numerous smaller reef fish and juveniles.

Swim farther out to find healthy hard corals and perhaps a resting lizardfish.

Legend of the Faros

Faro reef systems resemble open-ocean atolls, featuring steep coral buttresses that enclose a central lagoon. In fact, the faro is referred to as a *shelf atoll*, or an atoll that develops on the continental shelf. Laughing Bird Caye is perched on the eastern ridge of just such a faro structure, one of only a handful in the world. As such, it's protected within both Laughing Bird Caye National Park and the Belize Barrier Reef Reserve System World Heritage Site.

Deep channels ring the caye, separating it from the mainland, the barrier reef and other cayes. The outer edge of the faro sports lush sponges, gorgonians and hard-coral growth, including staghorn and elkhorn corals in interlocking thickets. Within the faro are patch reefs and coral ridges that host a tremendous diversity of fish and invertebrate life. The nearshore waters are ideal for both snorkeling and diving.

29 Laughing Bird Caye South

A soft mixture of silt and sand, the seabed here is easily disturbed. Depending on tides and prevailing winds, visibility ranges from about 20 to 100ft or more. Even in less-than-perfect conditions, however, the site offers unique features and a welcome contrast to wall dives along the barrier reef.

The bottom slopes gradually away from the caye to about 25ft, where healthy gorgonians and sponges flourish atop brain, star and mushroom corals.

Location: .5 mile (.8km) SE of Laughing Bird Caye

Depth Range: 25-65ft (8-20m)

Access: Boat

Expertise Rating: Novice

As you head deeper, search amid the gorgonians and sponges to find an array of anemones, tunicates, roving invertebrates and juvenile fish. Many species of commensal shrimp, crabs and small fish inhabit the anemones and corals—enough to keep a macrophotographer or marine biologist happy for hours.

Squat anemone shrimp shelter amid their host's protective tentacles.

30　North Wall

This stretch of the barrier reef is largely submerged, with only the occasional patch breaking the surface. You'll begin this dive in 25ft atop the shelf and meander amid coral outcrops and swaying gorgonians to the edge of the wall at 50ft, which plunges to great depths. The current can be quite strong here. Simply go with the flow while your boat tracks you from the surface.

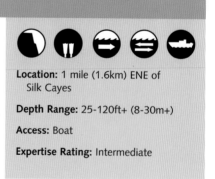

Location: 1 mile (1.6km) ENE of Silk Cayes

Depth Range: 25-120ft+ (8-30m+)

Access: Boat

Expertise Rating: Intermediate

The wall is peppered with large barrel sponges and branching gorgonians, which reach into the current to feed. The current also attracts tightly bunched shoals of horse-eye and yellow jacks, dog snappers and schoolmasters. A narrow sandy shelf at 120ft marks your turnaround point. Gradually work your way back to the shallows for a safety stop above the lush gorgonian fields.

31 Silk Cayes (Queen Cayes)

Locals and some maps may refer to this scattering of small, picture-postcard islands as the Queen Cayes, although either name is acceptable. A lunchtime break on one of the islands provides a chance for a gentle snorkel or shallow dive. Many dive centers take students here for their first open-water dives. The site offers a relaxing contrast to nearby high-energy wall dives and is a great opportunity for photographers to record some of the smaller reef fish species. Be careful when entering and exiting the water, as the shallows are full of black spiny urchins.

Fringed with turtle grass and coral heads, the bright, sandy shallows serve as a nursery for juvenile species. Dense shoals of baitfish, juvenile spadefish and

Location: 22 miles (35km) ESE of Placencia

Depth Range: Surface-20ft (6m)

Access: Boat or shore

Expertise Rating: Novice

tiny jacks swirl in a foot of water. This moving feast in turn attracts hungry barracuda and halfbeaks, which edge closer and closer inshore, determined to feed on the fry. Swim farther out amid the developing coral heads to find colorful pairs of butterflyfish and iridescent stoplight parrotfish, which graze on algae.

These tiny cayes offer a break between dives for snorkeling or a picnic on the beach.

32 Silk Cayes Canyons

As the reef table runs south, small coral outcrops alternate with low patch reefs. These coalesce into spurs and grooves along the edge of the drop-off. At this site some gullies are quite deep, reaching 90ft or so before tumbling over the wall. You'll find a variety of healthy hard corals and gorgonians, though the reef is frequently pounded by heavy oceanic swells. Even in calm conditions there's noticeable water movement, and a 4 to 6ft surface swell translates to heavy surge

Location: 1.5 miles (2.4km) ESE of Silk Cayes

Depth Range: 25-130ft+ (8-40m+)

Access: Boat

Expertise Rating: Intermediate

below. Conditions improve at depth, but divers face a struggle in the shallows if the weather turns rough.

The wall attracts many pelagic species, and reef sharks are common visitors. You're also likely to encounter groups of odd-looking gray ocean triggerfish, which tow remoras almost as large as themselves and are often accompanied by striped pilotfish.

Consider yourself lucky if you spot a Caribbean reef shark.

MICHAEL LAWRENCE

33 Pompion Caye Wall

This dive starts in about 25ft on a broad shallow reef shelf, which gradually slopes to 45ft amid healthy hard corals and branching gorgonians atop the wall. Watch your depth, as the wall plunges well below the sport-diving limit. While coral and sponge growth on the reef face is somewhat sporadic, you will find plenty of pelagics and big fish.

Location: 1 mile (1.6km) east of Pompion Caye

Depth Range: 25-100ft+ (8-30m+)

Access: Boat

Expertise Rating: Intermediate

Search amid the sponges and gorgonians to find such surprises as this green moray.

Barracuda visit cleaning stations along the wall, while schools of Atlantic spadefish and cubera snappers patrol the blue. Large black groupers prefer to laze under overhangs with attendant remoras and ignore your approach. Finish your dive in the shallows, where an ever-present surge ranges from mild to quite heavy.

34 Pompion Caye

Pompion Caye is an idyllic tropical island with white sandy beaches fringed by palms and whose sole inhabitant is the local game warden. In the surrounding shallows snorkelers find anything from spotted eagle rays and moray eels to trunkfish, parrotfish and schools of sardines and baitfish, which fall prey to dive-bombing pelicans.

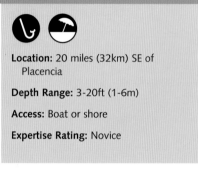

Location: 20 miles (32km) SE of Placencia

Depth Range: 3-20ft (1-6m)

Access: Boat or shore

Expertise Rating: Novice

Follow the sand flats out to turtle grass beds, which shelter several juvenile species. Beyond are numerous small coral heads and sea fans, home to a variety of reef fish. Pairs of hogfish scour the sand for small crustaceans, while bigger predators such as sleek tarpon and barracuda shadow the shoals of small fish.

Thousands of baitfish fill the shallows, attracting dive-bombing pelicans.

35 Chub Canyons

Just south of Pompion Caye Wall the reef flat develops into a low and narrow spur-and-groove formation, which slopes gradually from about 50 to 70ft. Ocean swells often bring heavy surge, though it's fairly manageable at depth.

The surge opens the door to hardy corals such as star, brain, mushroom and lettuce, as well as branching gorgonians, which mirror the water's motion. Follow the spurs to the drop-off, where you'll find schools of bluestriped grunts, horse-eye and yellow jacks and schoolmasters holding station in the gentle current.

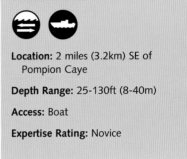

Location: 2 miles (3.2km) SE of Pompion Caye

Depth Range: 25-130ft (8-40m)

Access: Boat

Expertise Rating: Novice

After exploring the wall, follow the gullies west to the sandy shallows, where you may encounter resting nurse sharks. You can usually approach quite close.

Sapodilla Cayes Marine Reserve

Locals insist the Sapodilla Cayes are the most beautiful islands in Belizean waters. They're at the heart of a marine reserve that protects the southernmost section of the Belize Barrier Reef. The reserve covers 49 sq miles (125 sq km) and includes eight sand and mangrove cayes. Land comprises only 2% of the reserve. The remaining 98% includes shallow patch reefs, spur-and-groove formations, extensive seagrass beds and sandbanks. The largest island in the group is Hunting Caye, whose east coast boasts a shallow bay and spectacular beach, one of the main turtle nesting sites in Belize. Access is by day boat from Placencia, as there are no resorts on the cayes.

Offshore Atolls Dive Sites

There are only four atolls in the Western Hemisphere, and three of them are right here in Belize. They sit atop two parallel submerged mountain ridges separated by a deepwater channel. The Turneffe Islands and Glover's Reef are on one, while Lighthouse Reef lies farther east. Rising amid deep offshore water, they boast some of the most exciting wall diving in the region and promise excellent visibility. To dive here, consider one of three options—daytrips through a dive center on the mainland or offshore cayes, a package stay at one of the atoll-based resorts or a berth on a live-aboard boat.

Turneffe Islands

A loose band of tropical cayes capped with verdant palms, shrubs and mangroves, the Turneffe Islands comprise the largest of the offshore atolls (30 miles/48km long and 10 miles/16km wide). About 19 miles (30km) from the mainland, the atoll is easily accessible via daytrip boats from Belize City, Ambergris Caye and Caye Caulker and is a popular first stop for the live-aboard fleet. While three atoll-based resorts offer diving services, the choice of sites is extensive, and you're unlikely to encounter another boat on your chosen site. Most dive sites are grouped around the south end and west side of the atoll, sheltered from the steady northeast trade winds—although the few exposed sites are among the most thrilling.

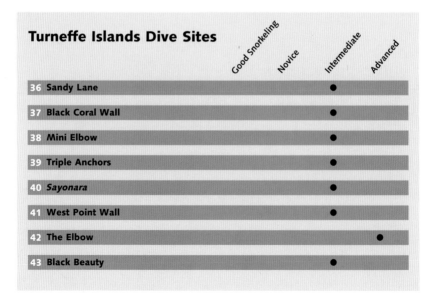

Turneffe Islands Dive Sites

	Good Snorkeling	Novice	Intermediate	Advanced
36 Sandy Lane			●	
37 Black Coral Wall			●	
38 Mini Elbow			●	
39 Triple Anchors			●	
40 Sayonara			●	
41 West Point Wall			●	
42 The Elbow				●
43 Black Beauty			●	

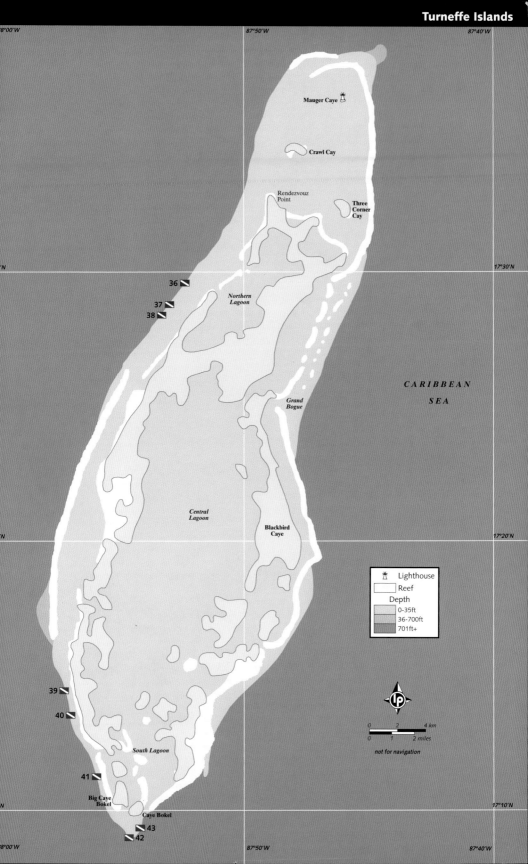

Mauger Caye

Crawl Cay

Rendezvouz
Point

Three
Corner
Cay

*Northern
Lagoon*

CARIBBEAN

SEA

Grand
Bogue

*Central
Lagoon*

Blackbird
Caye

Lighthouse

Reef

Depth

0-35ft

36-700ft

701ft+

South Lagoon

Big Caye
Bokel

Caye Bokel

not for navigation

Coral Rings

Millions of years ago as volcanic islands rose from the sea, corals took hold along their shorelines, forming protective fringing reefs. As time passed, the islands succumbed to erosion and changes in sea level, slowly slipping beneath the waves. But the corals continued to grow, reaching toward the life-sustaining sunlight. Capped with sandy islands, these familiar coral atolls now ring scattered patch reefs amid shallow lagoons.

GREG JOHNSTON

The Turneffe Islands cap a coral atoll that encircles a shallow central lagoon.

36 | Sandy Lane

About 50 minutes by boat from the mainland, this site is on the northwest side of the atoll, sheltered from prevailing winds. The dive starts beneath the mooring in 40ft and is typically done as a drift dive, despite the lack of currents. You'll swim south over a gently sloping reef, which bottoms out on a series of sandy ledges and a plateau between 80 and 100ft.

Branching gorgonians stand out amid healthy hard corals along the

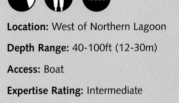

Location: West of Northern Lagoon

Depth Range: 40-100ft (12-30m)

Access: Boat

Expertise Rating: Intermediate

slope. Although algae growth spread in the wake of Hurricane Keith in October 2000, there's no sign of significant damage. Search the many nooks, crannies and overhangs for a wide variety of invertebrates, including large lobsters, crabs and banded coral shrimp. Amid the corals and sponges you'll find purple-tipped giant anemones, home to Pederson cleaning shrimp and tiny porcelain crabs.

Farther south the slope is more pronounced and sports large tube sponges. Fish life here is varied and active, with occasional visits from large pelagics.

37 Black Coral Wall

Just south of Sandy Lane, this site offers similar topography, though a number of sizable spurs lead toward the wall, and the drop here is more pronounced. Sponge and coral growth are also similar. Despite the site name, black coral is not prolific, though you'll find plenty of gorgonians. Black coral has long been a commercial target for the jewelry trade, so this might explain its scarcity here.

That aside, marine life is thriving, with all the usual suspects, including large shoals of schoolmasters along the edge of the drop-off between 50 and 60ft. As you work your way back to the reeftop, look for macro life such as

Location: West of Northern Lagoon

Depth Range: 30-130ft (9-40m)

Access: Boat

Expertise Rating: Intermediate

grazing nudibranchs and flatworms, as well as giant anemones with attendant shrimp and the pretty diamond blenny. You'll also spot lots of boxfish and trunkfish, particularly buffalo trunkfish, which often cruise in pairs above the reef with small remoras.

Being resourceful or perhaps just lazy, a remora hitches a ride on a buffalo trunkfish.

38 Mini Elbow

Though moorings mark this site, it's generally conducted as a drift drive. You'll descend on a gentle sandy slope with scattered coral heads. These gradually coalesce into a more continuous reef structure, with deep cuts running west. Follow one of the cuts to the edge of the wall, between 80 and 100ft.

To the south is the small namesake promontory in the wall, where turbulence attracts jacks and tarpon. Look for several large green morays amid the sponges along the edge of the drop-off. Deeper on the wall you'll find large sea fans, which stretch into the blue to feed.

Location: West of Northern Lagoon

Depth Range: 30-100ft+ (9-30m+)

Access: Boat

Expertise Rating: Intermediate

The shallows attract schools of creole wrasses, which cruise atop the reef, descending en masse every few minutes to feed. Turtles are also common here, especially in summer, when they gather to lay eggs onshore.

Gorgonians and sponges grow thick along the drop-off.

39 Triple Anchors

This site is named for a trio of coral-encrusted 18th century anchors, one close to the mooring pin in 45ft. Have your divemaster show you the other two. Large reef patches and outcrops dot a sandy slope that leads to the wall at 100ft or so. You'll find very large barrel and tube sponges on the sand. Coral overhangs in the shallows are home to spiny lobsters, while branching gorgonians shelter trumpetfish and timid snappers. Follow the edge of the drop-off to spot passing pairs of majestic eagle rays.

Location: SW side of atoll

Depth Range: 45-100ft+ (14-30m+)

Access: Boat

Expertise Rating: Intermediate

Back on the reeftop, one or two big barracuda will show off their teeth while you make your safety stop. At night your boat's lights may attract tarpon, which race in from the black to snap up baitfish.

You'll find especially long yellow tube sponges in the shallows.

40 *Sayonara*

A small passenger and cargo shuttle that served Turneffe Island Lodge, the *Sayonara* was deliberately sunk here in 1985. The ship is now well broken up, although you can still distinguish its basic shape. She lies on a bed of sand and coral rubble at 50ft.

Location: SW side of atoll

Depth Range: 30-100ft+ (9-30m+)

Access: Boat

Expertise Rating: Intermediate

Yellowhead jawfish hover vertically.

Explore the wreck to find schools of small fish. The surrounding sand shelters many yellowhead jawfish, which hover above their burrows until you get too close. Male jawfish incubate the females' eggs in their mouths.

A gentle slope leads to the drop-off at 100ft or more. Large coral heads sport a variety of gorgonians, barrel and rope sponges. You'll spot lone barracuda and small shoals of jacks and yellowtail snappers, as well as pairs of tiny slender filefish amid the branching gorgonians.

41 West Point Wall

The mooring here is perched atop the edge of the wall, which drops sharply from only 25ft. Carved with deep cuts and gullies, the reeftop cries out to be explored. Save it for the latter half of your dive, after you've reached your target depth on the wall.

As you descend, you'll find a grand selection of colorful vase, rope and barrel sponges, which give way to stands of black coral and impressive deepwater sea fans. Big black groupers inspect you from fissures along the wall, while barracuda, spadefish and eagle rays shadow you from the blue.

Ascend to one of the gullies and follow it toward shallow water. Almost

Location: NW of Big Caye Bokel

Depth Range: 25-130ft (8-40m)

Access: Boat

Expertise Rating: Intermediate

forming tunnels in places, these cuts shelter lobsters, shoaling silversides, squirrelfish and the elusive toadfish. You'll emerge on broad sand patches interspersed with coral heads. Search the sand for peacock flounders, southern stingrays, yellowhead jawfish and colonies of swaying garden eels.

West Point Wall boasts colorful sponges along a steep drop-off.

42 The Elbow

On the south tip of the atoll, this is one of Turneffe's most-exposed sites. Even gentle winds stir up sizable swell, thus it's only diveable in calm conditions. It should always be approached as a drift dive with reliable surface cover, as the current could sweep divers into open water, particularly during a safety stop. You should also carry signaling equipment (e.g., a marker tube, flag, air horn, etc.) to aid pickup if you separate from the group.

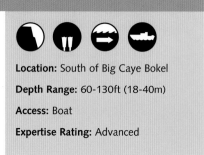

Location: South of Big Caye Bokel

Depth Range: 60-130ft (18-40m)

Access: Boat

Expertise Rating: Advanced

You'll drop in along the edge of the wall, where the reef rises to about 60ft, though most of the dive will be spent deeper and farther off the reef in open water. While limited, your bottom time will be unforgettable.

The namesake elbow is the point where currents that flow down both sides of the atoll converge. This turbulence attracts dense schools of crevalle and horse-eye jacks, Atlantic spadefish, barracuda and cubera snappers, as well as several shark species. Pods of dolphins are frequent visitors, and schools of eagle rays may pass by.

Strong currents attract jacks and snappers.

43 Black Beauty

Just east of The Elbow, this site also requires calm weather for a comfortable dive. When the winds are up, surge and swell are strong enough to break the moorings. When conditions allow, this is an excellent dive, offering frequent sightings of pelagics and sharks.

The dive typically starts in 50ft atop a coral buttress, which slopes sharply and is laced with gullies. It's exhilarating to follow one of these sandy chutes and emerge on the vertical wall at 100ft or so. Currents are often strong on the wall—start your tour against the flow for an easier return to the boat. The nutrient-

Location: SE of Big Caye Bokel

Depth Range: 50-130ft (15-40m)

Access: Boat

Expertise Rating: Intermediate

laden water supports rich sponge growth and numerous deepwater sea fans. As the site name implies, black coral was once prolific here, though not anymore. End your dive on the reeftop amid a healthy population of reef species.

Lighthouse Reef

Some 40 miles (64km) east of Belize City (at its closest point), Lighthouse Reef is the most seaward of the three atolls. Although the legendary Blue Hole may be the headline attraction, the region offers a wide variety of dive sites. Its offshore location means generally excellent visibility and frequent encounters with large marine denizens.

While you're here, visit the nature reserve on Half Moon Caye. You should also try snorkeling off the caye, particularly around the old wooden pier just east of the new quay. Rays and nurse sharks often rest here, and they'll come within reach if you're patient and move slowly.

Based on Northern Caye, Lighthouse Reef Resort is the atoll's sole accommodation. This upmarket resort boasts its own airstrip to receive guests from Belize City.

GREG JOHNSTON

At the heart of Lighthouse Reef is the world-renowned Blue Hole, a collapsed ancient cavern.

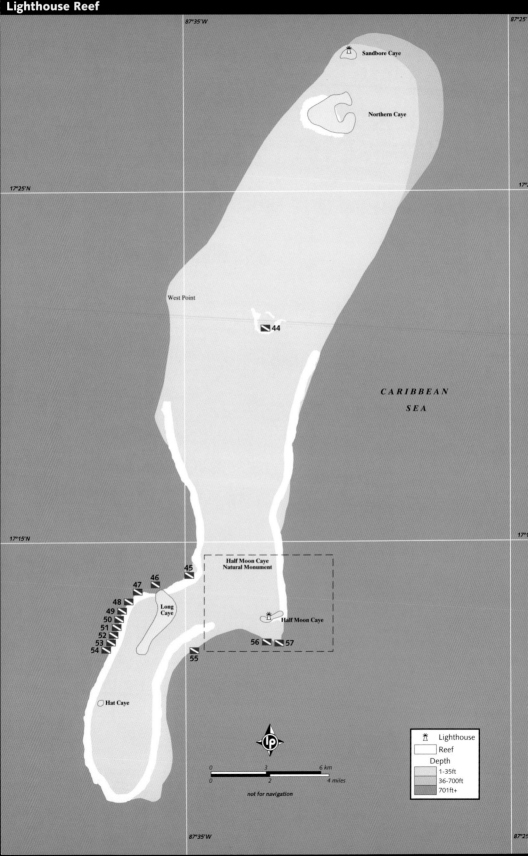

87°35'W

87°25'

Sandbore Caye

Northern Caye

17°25'N

17°

West Point

44

CARIBBEAN

SEA

17°15'N

17°1

45

Half Moon Caye
Natural Monument

46

47

48
49
50
51
52
53
54

Long
Caye

55

Half Moon Caye

56 57

Hat Caye

IP

| 0 | | 3 | | 6 km |
| 0 | | 2 | | 4 miles |

not for navigation

	Lighthouse
	Reef
Depth	
	1-35ft
	36-700ft
	701ft+

87°35'W

87°2

Lighthouse Reef Dive Sites

	Good Snorkeling	Novice	Intermediate	Advanced
44 Blue Hole	●			●
45 Eagle Ray Wall	●		●	
46 The Aquarium			●	
47 Silver Caves			●	
48 Painted Wall			●	
49 Julie's Jungle			●	
50 Quebrada			●	
51 Long Caye Ridge			●	
52 Pete's Palace			●	
53 Nurse Shark Ridge			●	
54 No Cocos (Tres Cocos)			●	
55 Elkhorn Forest			●	
56 Half Moon Wall			●	
57 Shark Point			●	

44 | Blue Hole

To best appreciate the size and symmetry of the Blue Hole, one should view it from a plane, though it's still very impressive as you boat across the center of this collapsed cave system. On first entering the water, you may be somewhat disappointed, as the visibility can be poor and the water has a gray cast to it. But after you descend through a thermocline at about 50 or 60ft, the water clears dramatically.

The sheer-sided wall drops about 100ft to the first undercut and stalactites. Although the water is clear, light levels are low as you wend your way through the formations. A good dive light is

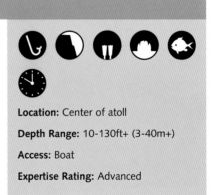

Location: Center of atoll

Depth Range: 10-130ft+ (3-40m+)

Access: Boat

Expertise Rating: Advanced

essential to appreciate the sponge and invertebrate life. Some of the local boats have been regularly chumming the waters on the south side of the hole to attract reef sharks, though you're unlikely to encounter any fish until you return to the rim. To be honest, once you've seen the first few stalactites, you've seen all the Blue Hole has to offer. While this is certainly an exciting, must-do site, one visit should be enough for most divers.

While there is some coral growth and fish life in the shallows, the reeftop can't compare to the atoll's spectacular outlying reefs, as water flow is limited in the surrounding shallow lagoon. To find the best snorkeling, swim away from the hole into the lagoon.

Massive stalactites below 100ft (30m) dwarf divers.

45 Eagle Ray Wall

This site is known for regular sightings of eagle rays, though as with most marine life encounters, this is a matter of luck. Whether or not you see one, this is a splendid dive. You'll start at the mooring pin in 30ft amid deeply cut reef outcrops, then drop over the sheer wall to a ledge between 115 and 145ft. You won't have to go this deep to find lush black coral trees,

Location: 1.5 miles (2.4km) north of Long Caye

Depth Range: 15-130ft+ (5-40m+)

Access: Boat

Expertise Rating: Intermediate

which grow along the overhangs and sport bright clusters of tunicates—an excellent macro subject. You'll encounter dense shoals of snappers and jacks along the wall, and perhaps a passing eagle ray or turtle.

The reeftop is rich in macro life. Many small purple sea fans host striking flamingo tongue cowries. You may also find nudibranchs and small fish species like triplefins and secretary blennies, which live in small holes in the reef. Swim toward shore to finish your dive in 15 to 18ft of water. The shallows offer good snorkeling and a chance to spot scorpionfish and peacock flounders.

46 The Aquarium

Here a well-developed spur-and-groove formation leads to the wall. The site is named for the wide variety of small resident reef fish on the reeftop and along the edge of the wall. When a current is running, you can shelter in one of the deep sandy gullies and closely observe the fish. This is a good site for photographers seeking cooperative subjects.

Location: NW corner of Long Caye

Depth Range: 25-130ft (8-40m)

Access: Boat

Expertise Rating: Intermediate

Turtles and bold French angelfish are common on the reef crest, while large black groupers and trumpetfish hover amid branching gorgonians atop the wall. Descend to about 60ft to find big barrel sponges and pretty azure vase sponges, which shelter banded coral shrimp and juvenile fish. Scan the blue water for such big fish as sharks and manta rays.

Check inside azure vase sponges to find banded coral shrimp.

47 Silver Caves

The mooring here is adjacent to the wall, which tops out at 30ft. Swimming over the edge, you'll find many colorful tube, barrel and rope sponges amid branching gorgonians, including broad deepwater sea fans, whose polyps are fully extended at night. Predatory tarpon and barracuda cruise the wall, while horse-eye jacks, bar jacks and chubs gather in large shoals beneath your boat.

The wall is peppered with numerous caves and overhangs, some home to dense shoals of silversides that part like a shimmering curtain as you swim through them, hence the site name. Take care when exploring the caves and bring a dive light to help you locate nocturnal species and appreciate the colorful encrusting organisms.

Location: NW of Long Caye

Depth Range: 20-130ft (6-40m)

Access: Boat

Expertise Rating: Intermediate

Spend your safety stop meandering atop the shallow coral gardens in 20ft. This site is worth several dives. Night dives are particularly rewarding. You'll encounter all manner of sleeping fish, foraging spiny lobsters, arrow crabs, brittle stars, sponges dotted with red night shrimp and tiny hermit crabs, as well as the inevitable marauding tarpon, which hunt in the beam of the boat's lights.

49 Painted Wall

As at all sites off Long Caye, this is approachable as either a wall dive or a leisurely tour of the reeftop. A shallow spur-and-groove formation runs along the top of the wall, with one or two deeper outlying cuts. When surface winds stir up strong surge in the shallows, head straight for deeper water. The wall itself drops sharply and is adorned with tall tube and stovepipe sponges alongside random tangles of red and deep purple rope and finger sponges. You'll spot many deepwater sea fans, especially under the overhangs. Inspect the fans closely to find tiny clingfish and clusters of vibrant purplish-blue tunicates.

Black groupers, pairs of French angelfish and turtles visit the wall, but

Location: West of Long Caye

Depth Range: 25-130ft (8-40m)

Access: Boat

Expertise Rating: Intermediate

the real fish activity happens in the shallows. Look for bizarre scrawled cowfish and pairs of whitespotted filefish, both of which can change their pattern and color. A mob of horse-eye jacks, Bermuda chub and the odd barracuda is usually awaiting divers back at the boat. Photographers are able to closely approach these fish, which seem to accept them into the pack.

Painted Wall is adorned with a variety of colorful sponges.

49 Julie's Jungle

This site was named after a marine biologist who helped install the mooring pin, which sits on the reeftop in 30ft. From there deep grooves run to the edge of a steep drop-off at 50ft. You'll spot big barrel sponges atop the wall, and once over the crest you'll find clusters of colorful tube sponges and branching gorgonians.

Location: West of Long Caye

Depth Range: 30-100ft (9-30m)

Access: Boat

Expertise Rating: Intermediate

Schools of horse-eye jacks cruise the edge of the wall and gather beneath dive boats with the usual large lone barracuda. Small shoals of grunts, snappers, creole wrasses and various angelfish buzz about the shallows. Ideal macro subjects, secretary blennies peer quizzically at divers from tiny holes in hard corals and barrel sponges. Living amid the many anemones are tiny purple Pederson cleaning shrimp, which will give you a manicure if you're patient.

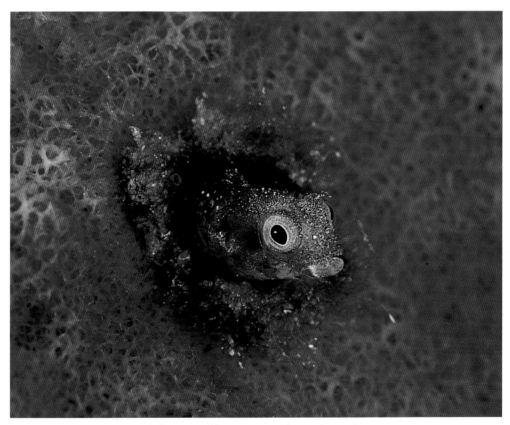

A curious little secretary blenny peeps out from its burrow in a sponge.

How Do They Keep So Clean?

One of the more fascinating finds on any reef is a cleaning station. All fish accumulate parasites, dead skin and scales, as well as small wounds and infections that require the ministrations of others. The best way to spot a cleaning station is to look for unusual behavior from resident fish. They may change color, hover vertically or open their mouths wide. Another giveaway is a grouping of fish that are normally predator and prey. Cleaning stations are widely treated as neutral territory, and hostilities are put on hold while fish wait patiently for attention. Approach slowly to get close to the action, and if you spot shrimp waiting for clients, try offering your hand for a one-minute manicure.

Cleaner shrimp, gobies and juvenile fish live in a variety of habitats. Pederson and spotted cleaner shrimp set up office in corkscrew, branching and giant anemones, while peppermint and scarlet-striped cleaner shrimp live in sponges, often devoting their efforts to a single green moray or black grouper. The larger banded coral shrimp also live amid sponges and cater to big fish. Cleaner gobies gather in small groups atop stony corals, sometimes with six or more working on a single fish. Wrasses are also regular cleaners, while juvenile Spanish hogfish and angelfish are occasional hygienists.

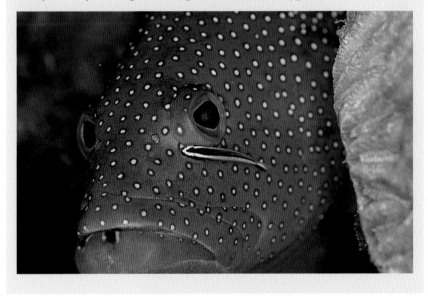

50 Quebrada

Quebrada ("gorge" in Spanish) refers to a wide sandy ravine that breaks the reef at this point. Your boat will moor in sand on a reef table peppered with small coral outcrops. The passage itself leads past coral buttresses to the sheer wall, which boasts lush coral formations along its overhanging edge.

Location: West of Long Caye

Depth Range: 25-130ft (8-40m)

Access: Boat

Expertise Rating: Intermediate

As you explore several deep overhangs along the wall, you'll notice a sandy ledge below you at 135ft. Forgo pushing to this depth, as there's plenty to see between 60 and 80ft. Resident dolphins often approach divers in pairs, making several close passes before disappearing into the blue. Have your camera ready, as trying to keep up with them would just leave you feeling inadequate.

You'll find a range of common reef species atop the wall and amid the shallow coral outcrops. Yellowtail snappers are particularly persistent, having been fed here in the past. The prospect of food means these and other fish stick close to divers, making them much easier to photograph. Also keep an eye out for invertebrates such as arrow and clinging crabs, banded coral shrimp and several nudibranch species.

Yellowtail snappers associate visiting divers with food.

51 Long Caye Ridge

The spurs here are widely spaced, with broad sand chutes that slope sharply toward the wall. Although you'll find patches of healthy brain, plate and staghorn coral, hard corals in the shallows show signs of wave damage, possibly due to hurricanes. The hard corals improve as you approach the edge of

Location: West of Long Caye

Depth Range: 25-100ft (8-30m)

Access: Boat

Expertise Rating: Intermediate

the wall, where you'll also find familiar arrays of sponges and branching gorgonians.

Moreover, where the coral is damaged or dead, algae now flourishes, attracting grazing angelfish, butterflyfish, hamlets and schools of blue tangs. Conditions are also ideal for spotting nudibranchs. Watch for scorpionfish, which keep well hidden amid the algae.

As you descend, watch carefully for the mottled patterns of venomous scorpionfish.

52 Pete's Palace

This site was named after live-aboard operator Peter Hughes, who placed the original mooring. An impressive series of deep spurs and grooves runs toward the drop-off, which tops out around 65ft. The wall is festooned with a selection of barrel and tube sponges, which fight for space in places.

Along the wall you'll spot lots of small reef fish and several cleaning stations, where bold black groupers will stare you down. Toward the end of your dive explore the shallows to find hermit crabs, lizardfish, peacock flounders and yellowhead jawfish. Very lucky divers may spot the elusive shortnose batfish.

Location: SW of Long Caye

Depth Range: 30-130ft (9-40m)

Access: Boat

Expertise Rating: Intermediate

This is another very good night dive. Look for sleeping boxfish, scrawled filefish and a number of nudibranch species. Your boat's lights will likely attract dense balls of baitfish, which in turn draw hungry barracuda, tarpon and squid.

53 Nurse Shark Ridge

Nurse Shark Ridge was named following numerous sightings of these fish. Atop the wall, broad sand patches border large coral heads, offering plenty of low overhangs where nurse sharks like to nap. Investigate the overhangs at the start of your dive for the best chance at seeing a shark before other divers disturb it. Just remember, there are no guarantees.

Location: SW of Long Caye

Depth Range: 40-130ft (12-40m)

Access: Boat

Expertise Rating: Intermediate

Peer beneath overhangs to find resting nurse sharks.

Anyway, there's plenty more to see along the wall. You'll often encounter a steady current, which attracts pelagics and other big fish. Check around the coral heads for prowling tarpon, which wait to pounce on small fish struggling against the current. Palometas also frequent the wall. Sporting long trailing dorsal and anal fins, these silvery jacks dodge in and out of the current in small groups of eight to a dozen.

54 No Cocos (Tres Cocos)

This site was originally named Tres Cocos, after three large coconut palms visible on the beach at Long Caye. Alas, hurricanes have since uprooted the landmarks, and now it's down to No Cocos, although some divemasters may still refer to the old name.

The mooring borders a lush coral garden, but don't linger here at first. Instead, drop down the adjacent wall, which tops out at 40ft. Its sheer face sports impressive and colorful sponges, as well as some deep overhangs fringed with black coral trees. Check the overhangs for huge black groupers, and keep

Location: Off SW corner of Long Caye

Depth Range: 30-130ft (9-40m)

Access: Boat

Expertise Rating: Intermediate

an eye on the blue for jacks, Atlantic spadefish and the occasional reef shark.

Toward the end of your dive, tour the interesting patch-and-gully formation in the shallows. You'll find cleaning stations hosted by juvenile hogfish, which seem partial to barracuda and green morays as clients. Abundant algae growth attracts small schools of grazing creole wrasses, parrotfish, blue tangs and hogfish.

Palms or no palms, the wall at No Cocos sports beautiful clusters of sponges.

55 Elkhorn Forest

This dive features a dramatic wall and healthy coral—though sadly there's no sign of the namesake elkhorn coral. The atoll largely shelters the site from northeasterly winds. But swells from the east still wash over the reef, making conditions uncomfortable in the shallows. Exercise caution during your safety stop and on your return to the boat.

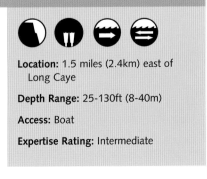

Location: 1.5 miles (2.4km) east of Long Caye

Depth Range: 25-130ft (8-40m)

Access: Boat

Expertise Rating: Intermediate

The reeftop is carpeted with swaying gorgonians that shelter all sorts of smaller fish. Dropping sheer from 50ft, the scalloped wall resembles small headlands and bays. You'll find spectacular plate and star corals, as well as several large barrel sponges that serve as cleaning stations staffed by juvenile Spanish hogfish. Watch patiently and you may see waiting fish chased off by territorial groupers that seem to want the cleaners all to themselves.

Pushy groupers dominate the cleaning stations.

56 Half Moon Wall

Divers can visit a spectrum of habitats at this popular site. Your boat will moor over sand flats that boast healthy beds of turtle grass and a garden eel colony. Beyond the turtle grass the sand slopes gently toward the reef. Scan this area carefully to spot southern stingrays either at rest or feeding on buried mollusks.

Deeply cut by gullies and swim-throughs, the reef is capped with healthy corals and busy with reef fish and small schools of bluestriped grunts. Follow the cuts through small caves and overhangs to the edge of the wall. You'll emerge between 70 and 80ft beside a sheer face covered with colorful sponges and gorgonians. Keep an eye out for manta and eagle rays, sharks and a variety of pelagics.

Location: South of Half Moon Caye

Depth Range: 30-130ft (9-40m)

Access: Boat

Expertise Rating: Intermediate

Spend the end of your dive exploring the sand and turtle grass. Parrotfish and hogfish root through the sand, followed by goatfish, triggerfish, gray angelfish, bar jacks and the occasional grouper, which pick up any remaining scraps. The garden eels are also worth a visit but are frustratingly shy if you're trying to photograph them.

You'll be in awe of the spectacular sponges and deepwater sea fans on Half Moon Wall.

Half Moon Caye Natural Monument

On the southeast corner of Lighthouse Reef, Half Moon Caye is home to the lighthouse that gave the atoll its name. You can visit this idyllic tropical island on a daytrip from Belize City or one of the cayes, and camping is available for the more adventurous. Rising barely 10ft (3m) above sea level, its 45 acres (18 hectares) comprise two distinct habitats.

Dominated by coconut palms, the east end is otherwise sparsely vegetated. Here

TOM BOYDEN

you'll find the remains of the original lighthouse and the current solar-powered model, as well as the rustic visitors center.

In contrast, the west end is lush, capped with mangroves that serve as a rookery for a variety of tropical and marine birds. From a treetop-level viewing platform you can watch adult red-footed boobies display as their chicks demand attention from the nest. There's also an entertaining nature walk through the center of the island, where you can observe a variety of smaller colorful birds, as well as the occasional monitor lizard and large land-based hermit crab.

57 Shark Point

An extension of Half Moon Wall, this reef shares a similar structure and form. You'll begin atop a broad sandy shelf, where southern stingrays nose in the sand for mollusks and crustaceans. Follow the gentle slope toward the coral reef atop the wall.

The reef buttresses here are tightly grouped, forming narrow valleys crowded with sea whips, sponges and reef fish. Choose one of the broader grooves and swim toward the wall. You'll emerge between 60 and 70ft over a sheer drop into the deep blue. While you may be lucky enough to spot reef sharks or even a hammerhead, you'll more likely see crevalle jacks, Spanish mackerel or perhaps eagle rays. Fed by gentle east-west

Location: SE of Half Moon Caye

Depth Range: 30-130ft (9-40m)

Access: Boat

Expertise Rating: Intermediate

currents, the corals, sea fans and sponges here are as spectacular as those on Half Moon Wall.

To finish the dive, make your way to the reeftop and drift back with the current. Look for schools of bluestriped grunts amid the gorgonians and stop to catch the action at one of the many cleaning stations.

The current-swept grooves at Shark Point support healthy sponge growth.

Glover's Reef

Some 25 miles (40km) southeast of Dangriga, Glover's Reef is Belize's southern-most atoll, capped by a collection of six small cayes that boast white-sand beaches backed by swaying palm trees. The atoll was named after 18th century English buccaneer John Glover, who used the cayes as a base for attacking Spanish merchant ships.

Only accessible by boat, the atoll boasts spectacular hard-coral formations that make a dive trip here worth the extra effort. Daytrips to Glover's Reef are available from Dangriga, Hopkins, Sittee River, Tobacco Caye and South Water Caye, while live-aboard boats only occasionally visit the atoll. The trip is weather dependent, so if you're determined to explore the best sites, stay at one of the resident resorts.

Four resorts are based on the atoll, one on Northeast Caye, one on Long Caye and the other two on Southwest Caye. Don't expect much in the way of nightlife, as diving, fishing, watersports and the beach are the major draws.

Glover's Reef Dive Sites

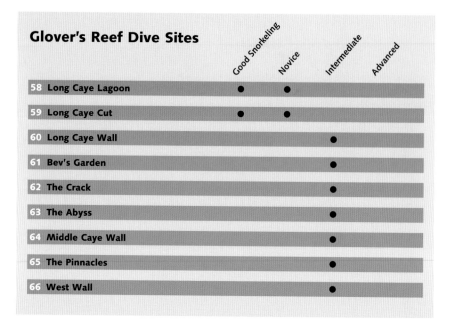

	Good Snorkeling	Novice	Intermediate	Advanced
58 Long Caye Lagoon	●	●		
59 Long Caye Cut	●	●		
60 Long Caye Wall			●	
61 Bev's Garden			●	
62 The Crack			●	
63 The Abyss			●	
64 Middle Caye Wall			●	
65 The Pinnacles			●	
66 West Wall			●	

This remote atoll offers secluded cayes and white-sand beaches.

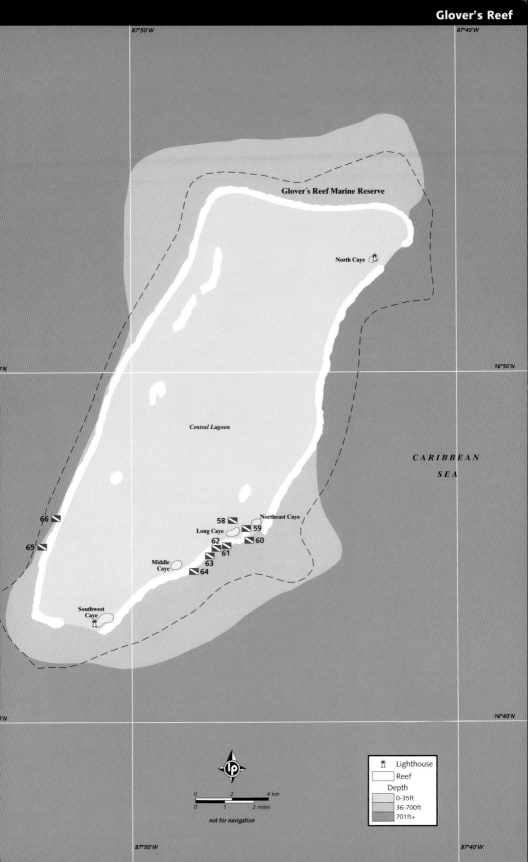

87°50'W

87°40'W

Glover's Reef Marine Reserve

North Caye

16°50'N

Central Lagoon

CARIBBEAN SEA

66

65

58
Northeast Caye
Long Caye
59
62
60
61
Middle Caye
63
64

Southwest Caye

16°40'N

87°50'W

87°40'W

0   2   4 km

0   1   2 miles

not for navigation

	Lighthouse
	Reef
	Depth
	0-35ft
	36-700ft
	701ft+

Glover's Reef Marine Reserve

Glover's Reef is the most geologically well developed of Belize's atolls. Its nearly unbroken reef line surrounds a shallow central lagoon dotted with hundreds of patch reefs and pinnacles. Steep drop-offs ring the atoll, plunging below 10,000ft (3,000m) to the east.

In addition to the atoll's underwater treasures, the cayes are also prized. The Belize government has established a marine research station on Middle Caye, while archaeologists have discovered the ruins of an ancient Mayan settlement on Long Caye.

A bird sanctuary was established at Glover's Reef in 1954, followed in 1978 by a United Nations recommendation that the entire atoll be declared an underwater preserve. Finally, in 1993 the atoll was declared a marine reserve.

58 Long Caye Lagoon

Lagoon dives offer a relaxing alternative to sites along the wall. You can swim out from the beach to explore nearshore turtle grass beds and coral heads or take a short boat ride to check out patch reefs farther inside the lagoon. Juvenile fish and specialized hunters swirl amid clusters of healthy shallow-water corals and gorgonians. Watch for shoals of sprats and tiny jacks, stingrays and eagle rays, grazing hogfish, dozens of conchs and slumbering nurse sharks.

If you dive or snorkel from the beach at Long Caye, have a look in the shallows beside the boat dock. They seem

Location: Off west side of Long Caye

Depth Range: 5-30ft (2-9m)

Access: Boat or shore

Expertise Rating: Novice

lifeless at first, but if you search amid the turtle grass and debris, you may spot seahorses, slender filefish, snake eels and a dozen or more juvenile spiny lobsters hiding in coconut shells and tin cans. You'll also encounter myriad tiny reef fish and bold barracuda.

Conchs carefully check out their surroundings before crawling across the sand.

59 Long Caye Cut

This site is ideal for snorkelers and student divers. It's also an excellent site for photographers, thanks to an abundance of adult and juvenile reef fish and the shallow depth, which allows long bottom times. While boat traffic is intermittent, this *is* one of the major channels into the lagoon—use caution as you ascend, and plan to surface beside one of the patch reefs that line the channel. Visibility can drop in the cut when a current is flowing from the lagoon.

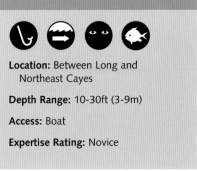

Location: Between Long and Northeast Cayes

Depth Range: 10-30ft (3-9m)

Access: Boat

Expertise Rating: Novice

The coral heads shelter all sorts of reef fish, including impressive morays, pairs of gray angelfish, queen triggerfish, and foureye and banded butterflyfish. Notice the often dramatic differences between adult and juvenile phases of the same species.

Southern stingrays and eagle rays feed on mollusks amid turtle grass beds and sand and rubble patches in mid-channel. Search the turtle grass to spot grazing conchs and their discarded shells, which shelter juvenile damselfish, wrasses and tobaccofish. This is also a good area to find the shortnose batfish.

Beauty & the Batfish

Some the oddest-looking fish are bottom dwellers that rely on camouflage to stalk their prey. Perhaps the most bizarre of this group is the shortnose batfish, *Ogcocephalus nasutus*. Its warty, almost triangular body sits atop stumpy fins that operate more like legs. Poor swimmers, batfish move by shuffling around on these fins. Below its extended snout is a doleful frown that appears smeared with red lipstick. The "nose" itself is in fact a lure. Lying motionless in the sand, the batfish gently twitches this lure to attract unwary small fish, which are quickly snapped up.

These peculiar fish are both rare and difficult to find, though divers often spot batfish around Long Caye. Look amid patches of short seagrass and rippled sand both in the lagoon and atop the wall. Sharp eyes and patience are a must to find them, but batfish often linger in one location, so you may be able to revisit them over several dives.

60 Long Caye Wall

Jacques Cousteau once rated this one of the three best dives in the world. While that claim is up for debate, it remains a spectacular dive. From the mooring a broad sandy plane slopes gently to a wall capped by lush coral growth. Deep gullies then lead to a sheer face blanketed with bright orange elephant ear sponges, yellow tube sponges and large deepwater gorgonians. Peer into the inky blue to spot schools of crevalle jacks, tarpon and Atlantic spadefish. Watch your gauges, as it's easy to lose track of time and depth.

Save some air to explore the sandy shallows, an ideal spot for novice divers to perfect their buoyancy, though surface winds sometimes bring strong surge.

Location: Just offshore, east of Long Caye

Depth Range: 30-130ft (9-40m)

Access: Boat

Expertise Rating: Intermediate

Garden eels peek shyly from their burrows beside the wall, while southern stingrays and eagle rays root in the sand, followed by attendant bar jacks. Farther up the slope you may find shortnose batfish, peacock flounders, hermit crabs and sand tilefish.

Black crinoids cap a huge elephant ear sponge atop the wall.

61 Bev's Garden

Bev's Garden is named for one of the divemasters on Long Caye. Close to the mooring at 30ft is the namesake coral garden, with healthy patches of lettuce and staghorn corals. These hardy corals are able to withstand the moderate surge spawned by westerly ocean swells.

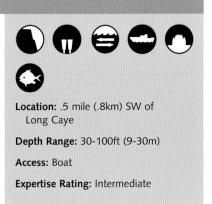

Location: .5 mile (.8km) SW of Long Caye

Depth Range: 30-100ft (9-30m)

Access: Boat

Expertise Rating: Intermediate

Follow the gentle slope toward the reef buttress, where dramatic cuts spill out along a sheer drop-off. The face sports big barrel and tube sponges, and you'll spot lots of reef fish and pelagics. Eagle rays are frequent visitors. Much of the wall is undercut between 60 and 70ft, in places forming small caves filled with silversides and groups of spiny lobsters.

Back up on the rim you'll find a number of cleaning stations hosted by juvenile Spanish hogfish and cleaner gobies—barracuda are favorite clients. Follow one of the cuts back to the coral garden, which is busy with small fish. Look for the tiny arrow blenny, which dwells in bore holes on the larger sponges.

62 The Crack

Shade-loving cup corals thrive in the tunnels.

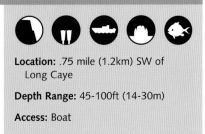

Location: .75 mile (1.2km) SW of Long Caye

Depth Range: 45-100ft (14-30m)

Access: Boat

Expertise Rating: Intermediate

A 10-minute boat ride from Long Caye, this site offers a foray into cave diving. The reef buttress is cut with narrow slots that meet near the reeftop, forming tunnels. One in particular, The Crack, opens at 45ft and falls steeply, exiting on the wall between 90 and 100ft. To either side of the tunnel entrance are small caves, overhangs and gullies that shelter schooling silversides and blackbar soldierfish and groups of inquisitive spiny lobsters.

The tunnel is quite narrow in places, with a sandy bottom that attracts sleepy nurse sharks—try not to startle them, as the only way out may be over your head! Although some sunlight does reach the tunnel, you should bring a dive light to better spot marine life in the recesses. You'll find bright orange *Tubastrea* cup corals, long sea whips, channel clinging crabs, shrimp and slipper lobsters.

Watch your depth as you emerge on the wall amid cruising horse-eye jacks and barracuda. To finish your dive, either ascend the reef face or follow another cut back to the shallows, though the latter option may be difficult if divers have disturbed the sand.

63 The Abyss

This site lies midway between Long and Middle Cayes. From the mooring you'll descend on numerous coral heads amid white-sand channels. Reaching toward the surface, the larger coral heads are festooned with lush gorgonians and clusters of long tube sponges. Toward the wall these heads merge and rise as steep buttresses, flanking deep sand chutes that lead to the drop-off.

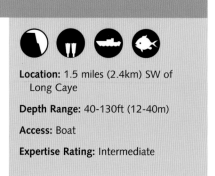

Location: 1.5 miles (2.4km) SW of Long Caye

Depth Range: 40-130ft (12-40m)

Access: Boat

Expertise Rating: Intermediate

Descend the sheer face to your target depth and drift either northeast or southwest in the gentle current. Almost every overhang is home to spiny lobsters and both spotted and green moray eels. Barracuda and groupers patrol beside sea fans, tangles of vivid rope sponges and several large barrel sponges, some big enough to hold a diver. This is *not* an invitation—any damage could ultimately kill the sponge. End your dive exploring the shallow reeftop.

64 Middle Caye Wall

Middle Caye is home to the Glover's Reef Marine Research Station, and the adjacent wall boasts some of the atoll's finest coral formations. Follow the sandy slope past scattered coral heads to the top of the wall at 50ft. Lined with gorgonians, the rim is marked by cuts and overhangs that conceal shoals of schoolmasters and bluestriped grunts. One overhang shelters an especially large green moray eel named Mordecai, which often shares its home with resting nurse sharks.

Location: Just east of Middle Caye

Depth Range: 30-130ft (9-40m)

Access: Boat

Expertise Rating: Intermediate

As you edge over the wall, you'll encounter a gentle current, which attracts schools of horse-eye jacks, Atlantic spadefish and silvery palometas. The visibility is often stunning here, so keep an eye on the blue water for passing reef sharks and logger-head turtles. The wall sports massive star and brain corals, which are festooned with long tube sponges, bright red and green rope sponges and deep-water sea fans that reach into the current. Throughout the site you'll observe hectic schools of creole wrasses and blue tangs, as well as pairs of bold French angelfish.

The wall is draped with sponges and deepwater sea fans.

65 | The Pinnacles

Dive operators usually skip the west side of Glover's Reef unless conditions are too rough out east. You'll need to prearrange the longer boat ride across the lagoon. There are no moorings—to find the sites, you'll need either the GPS coordinates or an experienced boatman. These sites are worth the extra effort.

This dive starts atop scattered coral heads in 40 to 50ft. Farther seaward, massive coral pinnacles rise from the lip of the wall to within 20ft of the surface. Between them are wide, gorgonian-lined

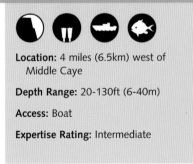

Location: 4 miles (6.5km) west of Middle Caye

Depth Range: 20-130ft (6-40m)

Access: Boat

Expertise Rating: Intermediate

sand channels, home to schoolmasters and bluestriped grunts. The channels exit on the sheer face amid colorful sponges and deepwater gorgonians. Expect to find schools of Spanish mackerel, trevallies, barracuda and glasseye snappers. Sharks often pass through, and manta rays visit the wall in the spring.

In such clear water, it's easy to stray deeper than you intend. Most divemasters suggest a conservative dive profile, as you're far from the nearest recompression chamber.

Wend your way between the pinnacles through gorgonian-lined sand channels.

66 West Wall

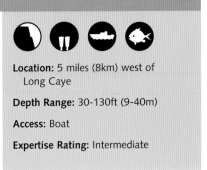

This area boasts several impressive sites that share similar topography. West Wall is one of the few with an official name. You'll swim down a sandy slope in 30ft past scattered coral heads. These gradually coalesce into broad coral buttresses that rise to within 30ft of the surface. Only the shallowest corals show signs of damage from past hurricanes. You'll find such abundant fish life and coral growth that it's possible to spend the whole dive exploring the reeftop.

The alternative is to follow one of several cuts in the wall that emerge over the blue-black depths at 70ft. Explore undercuts filled with gorgonians and sponges to find schools of blackbar soldierfish, but keep an eye on the blue for larger denizens. To finish your dive, head back through an adjacent cut or ascend to the rim and explore the shallow reeftop.

Location: 5 miles (8km) west of Long Caye

Depth Range: 30-130ft (9-40m)

Access: Boat

Expertise Rating: Intermediate

Blackbar soldierfish emerge from reef crevices at dusk.

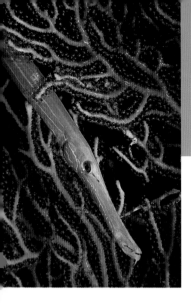

Marine Life

The waters that ring the Belize Barrier Reef and offshore atolls host nearly every species of fish and coral found throughout the Caribbean. The reefs also support an amazing variety of colorful sponges in all sizes and shapes, including stovepipes, barrels, elephant ears, ropes, vases and candelabras. Colors range from pastel pinks and purples to vivid greens, yellows and reds. The sponges, together with the hard corals and gorgonians, provide shelter and habitat to more than 600 species of fish and invertebrates.

While it would be impractical to list all the species you are likely to see while diving in Belize, this section will identify some of the more common vertebrates and invertebrates. The next section describes potentially harmful or dangerous marine life you may encounter.

Common names are used freely by most divers but are often inconsistent. The two-part scientific name is more precise. This system is known as binomial nomenclature—the method of using two words (shown in italics) to identify an organism. The first italic word is the genus, into which members of similar species are grouped. The second word, the species, refers to a recognizable group within a genus whose members are capable of interbreeding.

Common Vertebrates

hawksbill turtle
Eretmochelys imbricata

sharptail eel
Myrichthys breviceps

sand diver
Synodus intermedius

longspine squirrelfish
Holocentrus rufus

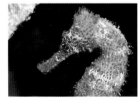

longsnout seahorse
Hippocampus reidi

graysby
Cephalopholis cruentatus

indigo hamlet
Hypoplectrus indigo

harlequin bass
Serranus tigrinus

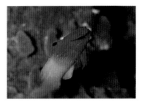

fairy basslet
Gramma loreto

palometa
Trachinotus goodei

schoolmaster
Lutjanus apodus

porkfish
Anisotremus virginicus

French grunt
Haemulon flavolineatum

spotted drum
Equetus punctatus

banded butterflyfish
Chaetodon striatus

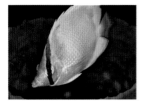

spotfin butterflyfish
Chaetodon ocellatus

gray angelfish
Pomacanthus arcuatus

rock beauty
Holacanthus tricolor

queen angelfish
Holacanthus ciliaris

blue chromis
Chromis cyanea

hogfish
Lachnolaimus maximus

queen parrotfish
Scarus vetula

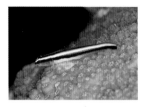

neon goby
Gobiosoma oceanops

peacock flounder
Bothus lunatus

whitespotted filefish
Cantherhines macrocerus

slender filefish
Monacanthus tuckeri

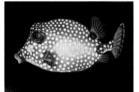

smooth trunkfish
Lactophrys triqueter

Common Invertebrates

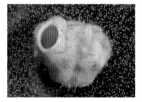

variable boring sponge
Siphonodictyon coralliphagum

yellow tube sponge
Aplysina fistularis

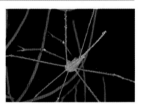

arrow crab
Stenarhynchus seticornis

blue bell tunicate
Clavelina puertosecensis

channel clinging crab
Mithrax spinosissimus

cushion sea star
Oreaster reticulatus

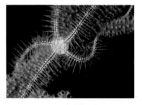

sponge brittle star
Ophiothrix suensonii

Christmas tree worm
Spirobranchus giganteus

West Indian sea egg
Tripneustes ventricosus

Hazardous Marine Life

Marine animals almost never attack divers, but many have defensive and offensive weaponry that can be triggered if they feel threatened or annoyed. The ability to recognize hazardous creatures is a valuable asset in avoiding injury. Following are some of the potentially hazardous creatures most commonly found in Belize.

Shark

Sharks come in many shapes and sizes. They are most recognizable by their triangular dorsal fin. Though many species are shy, such as the pictured nurse shark, there are occasional attacks. About 25 species worldwide are considered dangerous to humans. Sharks will generally not attack unless provoked, so don't taunt, tease or feed them. Avoid spearfishing, carrying fish baits or mimicking a wounded fish and your likelihood of being attacked will greatly diminish. Face and quietly watch any shark that is acting aggressively and be prepared to push it away with a camera, knife or tank. If someone is bitten by a shark, stop the bleeding, reassure the patient, treat for shock and seek immediate medical aid.

Barracuda

Barracuda are identifiable by their long, silver, cylindrical bodies and razorlike teeth protruding from an underslung jaw. They swim alone or in small groups, continually opening and closing their mouths, an action that looks daunting but actually assists their respiration. Though barracuda will hover near divers to observe, they are really somewhat shy, though they may be attracted by shiny objects that resemble fishing lures. Most recorded attacks by barracuda have been associated with fish feeding and spearfishing. Irrigate a barracuda bite with fresh water and treat with antiseptics, anti-tetanus and antibiotics.

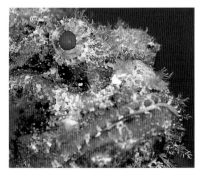

Scorpionfish

Scorpionfish are well-camouflaged creatures that have poisonous spines along their dorsal fins. They are often difficult to spot, since they typically rest quietly on the bottom or on coral, looking more like rocks. Practice good buoyancy control and watch where you put your hands. Scorpionfish wounds can be excruciating. To treat a puncture, wash the wound and immerse it in nonscalding hot water for 30 to 90 minutes.

Moray Eel

Distinguished by their long, thick, snakelike bodies and tapered heads, moray eels come in a variety of colors and patterns. Don't feed them or put your hand

in a dark hole—eels have the unfortunate combination of sharp teeth and poor eyesight and will bite if they feel threatened. If you are bitten, don't try to pull your hand away suddenly—the teeth slant backward and are extraordinarily sharp. Let the eel release it and then surface slowly. Treat with antiseptics, anti-tetanus and antibiotics.

Stingray

Identified by its diamond-shaped body and wide "wings," the stingray has one or two venomous spines at the base of its tail. Stingrays like shallow water and tend to rest on silty or sandy seafloors, often burying themselves in the sand. Often only the eyes, gill slits and tail are visible. These creatures are harmless unless you sit or step on them. Though injuries are uncommon, wounds are always extremely painful and often deep and infective. Immerse wound in nonscalding hot water and seek medical aid.

Jellyfish

Jellyfish sting by releasing nematocysts, stinging cells contained in their trailing tentacles. As a rule, the longer the tentacles, the more painful the sting. Stings

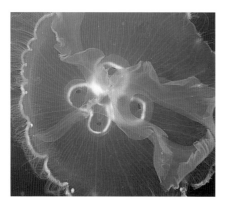

are often irritating and not painful but should be treated immediately with a decontaminant such as vinegar, rubbing alcohol, baking soda, papain or dilute household ammonia. A far greater threat is the Portuguese man-of-war, a distant cousin of the jellyfish that often floats at the surface and has very long trailing tentacles. Sting symptoms range from mild itch to intense pain, blistering, skin discoloration, shock, breathing difficulties and even unconsciousness. Remove the tentacles, preferably with tweezers, though anything but bare hands will do. Apply a decontaminant and seek immediate medical aid. Allergic reactions can be severe and life-threatening.

Bristle Worm

Also called fire worms, bristle worms are found on most reefs. They have segmented bodies covered with either tufts or bundles of sensory hairs that extend

in tiny, sharp, detachable bristles. If you touch one, the tiny stinging bristles lodge in your skin and cause a burning sensation that may be followed by a red spot or welt. Remove embedded bristles with adhesive tape, rubber cement or a commercial facial peel. Apply a decontaminant such as vinegar, rubbing alcohol or dilute ammonia.

Sea Urchin

Sea urchins tend to live in shallow areas near shore and come out of their shelters at night. They vary in coloration and size, with spines ranging from short and blunt to long and needle-sharp. The spines are the urchin's most dangerous weapon, easily able to penetrate neoprene wetsuits, booties and gloves. Treat minor punctures by extracting the spines and immersing the area in nonscalding hot water. More serious injuries require medical attention.

Fire Coral

Although often mistaken for stony coral, fire coral is a hydroid colony that secretes a hard, calcareous skeleton. Fire coral grows in many different shapes, often encrusting or taking the form of a variety of reef structures. It's usually identifiable by its tan, mustard or brown color and fingerlike columns with whitish tips. The entire colony is covered by tiny pores and fine, hairlike projections nearly invisible

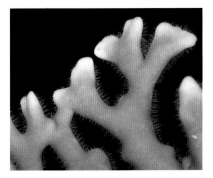

to the unaided eye. Fire coral "stings" by discharging small, specialized cells called nematocysts. Contact causes a burning sensation that lasts for several minutes and may produce red welts on the skin. Do not rub the area, as you'll only spread the stinging particles. Cortisone cream can reduce the inflammation, and antihistamine cream is good for killing the pain. A doctor should treat serious stings.

Diving Conservation & Awareness

The Belize government was quick to recognize the impact that diving and other marine activities could have on the country's reefs. Uncontrolled development would lead to pollution, overfishing and damage to the reefs from anchoring and increased diver traffic.

In 1981 the National Parks System Act was passed, spurring establishment of a series of natural monuments, wildlife sanctuaries, national parks and nature reserves. A dozen protected marine areas now safeguard the reef ecosystems. Seven of these regions are collectively listed as the Belize Barrier Reef Reserve System, a UNESCO World Heritage Site, while others are protected under local initiatives. Additional sites will be set aside as development warrants.

Marine Reserves & Regulations

Managed by the Fisheries and Forestry Departments, many of the reserves are zoned (some seasonally) to protect marine habitats, while still allowing reasonable economic benefit through fishing and tourism. Other critical marine habitats are wholly protected. Meanwhile, efforts are underway to mitigate watersports' impact on the health and condition of the reefs.

The most popular dive sites boast permanent moorings to prevent anchor damage, and divers are encouraged to take buoyancy control classes. It's also illegal to hunt turtles or collect corals or shells, even when found dead on the beaches. If you find these items for sale, please do not purchase them. Not only would that propagate the trade, you may also be detained and heavily fined by customs officials if such items are found in your baggage.

National Park Objectives

- Ensure the health of the fishery stock
- Regulate watersports
- Monitor reefs and assist researchers
- Provide jobs to tour guides and a venue for recreational activities
- Prohibit illegal fishing and deter other activities that may harm the reef
- Educate visitors about reef conservation and awareness

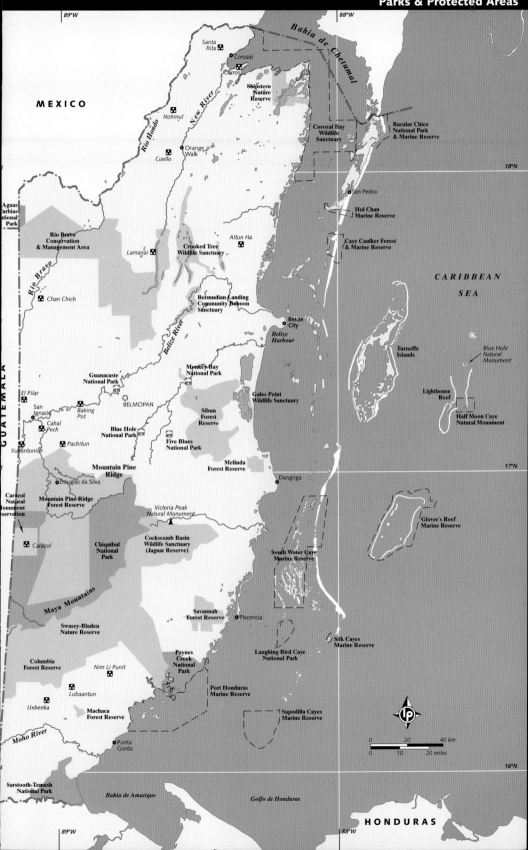

89°W

88°W

MEXICO

Bahía de Chetumal

Santa Rita

Corozal

Cerros

Shipstern Nature Reserve

Nohmul

Rio Hondo

New River

Corozal Bay Wildlife Sanctuary

Bacalar Chico National Park & Marine Reserve

Orange Walk

Cuello

18°N

Aguas Turbias National Park

San Pedro

Hol Chan Marine Reserve

Rio Bravo Conservation & Management Area

Lamanai

Crooked Tree Wildlife Sanctuary

Altun Ha

Caye Caulker Forest & Marine Reserve

CARIBBEAN SEA

Rio Bravo

Chan Chich

Bermudian Landing Community Baboon Sanctuary

Belize River

Belize City

Belize Harbour

Turneffe Islands

Blue Hole Natural Monument

Monkey Bay National Park

Guanacaste National Park

BELMOPAN

Gales Point Wildlife Sanctuary

Lighthouse Reef

El Pilar

San Ignacio

Baking Pot

Cahal Pech

Blue Hole National Park

Sibun Forest Reserve

Half Moon Caye Natural Monument

GUATEMALA

Pacbitun

Xunantunich

Five Blues National Park

Mountain Pine Ridge

Melinda Forest Reserve

17°N

Douglas da Silva

Dangriga

Caracol Natural Monument Reservation

Mountain Pine Ridge Forest Reserve

Victoria Peak Natural Monument

Glover's Reef Marine Reserve

Caracol

Chiquibul National Park

Cockscomb Basin Wildlife Sanctuary (Jaguar Reserve)

South Water Caye Marine Reserve

Maya Mountains

Swasey-Bladen Nature Reserve

Savannah Forest Reserve

Placencia

Silk Cayes Marine Reserve

Columbia Forest Reserve

Nim Li Punit

Paynes Creek National Park

Laughing Bird Caye National Park

Lubaantun

Uxbenka

Machaca Forest Reserve

Port Honduras Marine Reserve

Moho River

Punta Gorda

Sapodilla Cayes Marine Reserve

N

0   20   40 km

0   10   20 miles

16°N

Sarstooth-Temash National Park

Bahía de Amatique

Golfo de Honduras

HONDURAS

89°W

88°W

Responsible Diving

Dive sites are often along reefs and walls covered in beautiful corals and sponges. It only takes a moment—an inadvertently placed hand or knee, or a careless brush or kick with a fin—to destroy this fragile, living part of our delicate ecosystem. By following certain basic guidelines while diving, you can help preserve the ecology and beauty of the reefs:

1. Never drop boat anchors onto a coral reef and take care not to ground boats on coral. Encourage dive operators and regulatory bodies in their efforts to establish permanent moorings at appropriate dive sites.

2. Practice and maintain proper buoyancy control and avoid overweighting. Be aware that buoyancy can change over the period of an extended trip. Initially you may breathe harder and need more weighting; a few days later you may breathe more easily and need less weight. Tip: Use your weight belt and tank position to maintain a horizontal position—raise them to elevate your feet, lower them to elevate your upper body. Also be careful about buoyancy loss: As you go deeper, your wetsuit compresses, as does the air in your BC.

3. Avoid touching living marine organisms with your body and equipment. Polyps can be damaged by even the gentlest contact. Never stand on or touch living coral. The use of gloves is no longer recommended: Gloves make it too easy to hold on to the reef. The abrasion caused by gloves may be even more damaging to the reef than your hands. If you must hold on to the reef, touch only exposed rock or dead coral.

4. Take great care in underwater caves. Spend as little time within them as possible, as your air bubbles can damage fragile organisms. Divers

Marine life can be unpredictable—look but don't touch.

should take turns inspecting the interiors of small caves and beneath ledges to lessen the chances of damaging contact.

5. Be conscious of your fins. Even without contact, the surge from heavy fin strokes near the reef can do damage. Avoid full-leg kicks when diving close to the bottom and when leaving a photo scene. When you inadvertently kick something, stop kicking! It seems obvious, but some divers either panic or are totally oblivious when they bump something. When treading water in shallow reef areas, take care not to kick up clouds of sand. Settling sand can smother the delicate reef organisms.

6. Secure gauges, computer consoles and the octopus regulator so they're not dangling—they are like miniature wrecking balls to a reef.

7. When swimming in strong currents, be extra careful about leg kicks and handholds.

8. Photographers should take extra precautions, as cameras and equipment affect buoyancy. Changing f-stops, framing a subject and maintaining position for a photo often conspire to thwart the ideal "no-touch" approach on a reef. When you must use "holdfasts," choose them intelligently (e.g., use one finger only for leverage off an area of dead coral).

9. Resist the temptation to collect or buy coral or shells. Aside from the ecological damage, collection of marine souvenirs depletes the beauty of a site and spoils other divers' enjoyment.

10. Ensure that you take home all your trash and any litter you may find as well. Plastics in particular pose a serious threat to marine life.

11. Resist the temptation to feed fish. You may disturb their normal eating habits, encourage aggressive behavior or feed them food that is detrimental to their health.

12. Minimize your disturbance of marine animals. Don't ride on the backs of turtles or manta rays, as this can cause them great anxiety.

Marine Conservation Organizations

Coral reefs and oceans face unprecedented environmental pressures. The following groups are actively involved in promoting responsible diving practices, publicizing environmental marine threats and lobbying for better policies.

CORAL: The Coral Reef Alliance
☎ 510-848-0110
www.coralreefalliance.org

Cousteau Society
☎ 757-523-9335
www.cousteausociety.org

Ocean Futures
☎ 805-899-8899
www.oceanfutures.com

Project AWARE Foundation
☎ 949-858-7657
www.padi.com/aware

Reef Environmental Education Foundation
☎ 305-451-0312
www.reef.org

ReefKeeper International
☎ 305-358-4600
www.reefkeeper.org

Listings

Telephone Calls

To call Belize, dial the international access code for the country you are calling from (in the U.S. it is 011) + 501 (Belize's country code) + the 7-digit local number. Toll-free numbers (800, 866, 877 or 888) are accessible from the U.S. and, usually, Canada.

Belize Telecommunications Ltd. recently changed all telephone numbers in Belize to 7-digit numbers. To confirm any phone number, log on to the BTL website at www.btl.net.

Accommodations

You'll find a wide variety of accommodations throughout Belize, from full-service resorts to guesthouses and backpacker hostels. Divers can choose a resort with an attached dive center or one offering a package deal with an independent dive center.

Contact information for dedicated dive resorts follows under the heading Diving Services & Resorts. For information about accommodations on the Turneffe Islands, Lighthouse Reef , Glover's Reef and South Water Caye, see that section.

Belize City

Best Western Belize Biltmore Plaza
☎ 223-2302 fax: 223-2301
www.bestwestern.com
biltmore@btl.net

Princess Hotel & Casino
☎ 223-2670 fax: 223-2660
www.princessbelize.com
resprinces@btl.net

Radisson Fort George Hotel & Marina
☎ 223-3333 fax: 227-3820
toll-free ☎ 800-333-3333
www.radisson.com/belizecitybz
rdfgh@btl.net

Ambergris Caye

Barrier Reef Hotel
☎ 226-2075 fax: 226-2719
barriereef@btl.net

Belize Yacht Club Resort
☎ 226-2777 fax: 226-2768
toll-free ☎ 800-688-0402
www.belizeyachtclub.com
frontdesk@belizeyachtclub.com

Blue Tang Inn
☎ 226-2326 fax: 226-2358
toll-free ☎ 866-337-8203
www.bluetanginn.com
info@bluetanginn.com

Caribbean Villas
☎ 226-2715 fax: 226-2855
www.caribbeanvillashotel.com
c-v-hotel@btl.net

Caribe Island Resort
☎ 226-3233 fax: 226-3399
www.ambergriscaye.com/caribeisland
ccaribe@btl.net

Casa Solana
☎ 226-2100 fax: 226-2855
casasolana@btl.net

Coconuts Caribbean Hotel
☎ 226-3500/3677/3514 fax: 226-3501
www.coconutshotel.com
coconuts@btl.net

Conch Shell Hotel
☎ 226-2062 fax: 226-3849
www.ambergriscaye.com/conchshell
conchshell@btl.net

Corona del Mar Hotel
☎ 226-2055 fax: 226-2461
www.ambergriscaye.com/coronadelmar
corona@btl.net

Hideaway Sports Lodge
☎ 226-2141 fax: 226-2269
hideaway@btl.net

Ambergris Caye (continued)

Journey's End Resort
☎ 226-2173 fax: 226-2397
toll-free ☎ 800-460-5665
www.journeysendresort.com
info@journeysendresort.com

Mata Rocks Resort
☎ 226-2336 fax: 226-2349
toll-free ☎ 888-628-2757
www.matarocks.com
matarocks@btl.net

Mayan Princess
☎ 226-2778 fax: 226-2784
toll-free ☎ 800-850-4101
www.mayanprincesshotel.com
mayanprin@btl.net

Rock's Inn
☎ 226-2326 fax: 226-2358
rocks@btl.net

Royal Palm Villas
☎ 226-2148/2244 fax: 226-2329
www.royalpalminn.com
royalpalm@btl.net

Ruby's Hotel
☎ 226-2063 fax: 226-2434
rubys@btl.net

Sands Hotel
☎ 226-2510 fax: 226-2618
sandshotel@btl.net

San Pedro Holiday Hotel
☎ 226-2014/2103 fax: 226-2295
www.sanpedroholiday.com
holiday@btl.net

Sun Breeze Beach Hotel
☎ 226-2191 fax: 226-2346
toll-free ☎ 800-688-0191
www.sunbreeze.net
sunbreeze@btl.net

Sunset Beach Resort
☎ 226-3890 fax: 226-3891
www.sunsetbeachbelize.com
bananas@btl.net

Tropica Beach Resort
☎ 973-492-7690 fax: 973-492-7692
toll-free ☎ 888-778-9776
www.tropicabelize.com
vacation@tropicabelize.com

The Villas at Banyan Bay
☎ 226-3739 fax: 226-2766
www.banyanbay.com
banyanbay@btl.net

Caye Caulker

Anchorage Resort
☎ 226-0391 fax: 226-0304
anchorage@btl.net

Iguana Reef Inn
☎ 226-0213 fax: 226-0000
www.inguanareefinn.com
iguanareef@btl.net

Mara's Place
☎ 226-0156

Rainbow Hotel
☎ 226-0123 fax: 226-0172

Shirley's Guesthouse
☎ 226-0145 fax: 226-0264

www.shirleysguesthouse.com
shirley@btl.net

Tom's Hotel
☎ 226-0102

Tree Tops Guesthouse
☎ 226-0008 fax: 226-0115
www.treetopsbelize.com
treetops@btl.net

Tropical Paradise Hotel
☎ 226-0124 fax: 226-0225

Vega Inn
☎ 226-0142 fax: 226-0269
www.vega.com.bz
lifestyles@vega.com.bz

Dangriga

Jaguar Reef Lodge
☎ 520-2040 fax: 520-2091
toll-free ☎ 800-289-5756
www.jaguarreef.com
jaguarreef@aotws.com

Lillpat Sittee River Resort
☎/fax: 520-2019

www.lillpat.com
lillpat@btl.net

Pelican Beach Resort
☎ 522-2044 fax: 522-2570
www.pelicanbeachbelize.com
sales@pelicanbeachbelize.com

Tobacco Caye

Gaviota Coral Reef Resort
☎ 520-5032 fax: 661-252-5856
www.gaviotabelize.com
tvece@pacbell.net

Ocean's Edge Lodge
☎ 614-9633 or 281-894-0548
toll-free ☎ 1-800-967-8184
www2.symet.net/beltex
beltex@symet.net

Tobacco Caye (continued)

Reef's End Lodge
☎ 522-2419 fax: 522-2828
www.reefsendlodge.com
reefsend@btl.net

Tobacco Caye Lodge
☎ 520-5033 or 227-6247 fax: 227-5309
www.tclodgebelize.com
tclodge@btl.net

Placencia

Luba Hati
☎ 523-3402 fax: 523-3403
www.lubahati.com
lubahati@btl.net

Serenity Resort
☎ 523-3232 fax: 523-3231
www.serenityresort.com
serenity@btl.net

Diving Services & Resorts

The majority of dive operators in Belize are PADI affiliated and teach a variety of certification and specialty courses. Most rent a full range of well-maintained equipment from leading manufacturers and offer both daily and weekly package rates. Many are associated with a particular resort and also provide pickup service from neighboring hotels.

Belize City

Hugh Parkey's Belize Dive Connection
☎ 223-4526 fax: 223-0532
www.belizediving.com
hugh@belizediving.com

Sea Sports Belize
☎ 223-5505 fax: 223-7007
www.seasportsbelize.com
seasprtsbz@btl.net

Ambergris Caye

Adventures in Watersports
☎ 226-3706/3023 fax: 226-3707

Amigos del Mar
☎ 226-2706 fax: 226-2648
toll-free ☎ 800-345-9786
www.amigosdive.com
amigosdive@btl.net

Aqua Dives Belize
☎ 226-3415/3222 fax: 226-3414
toll-free ☎ 800-641-2994
www.aquadives.com
aquadives@btl.net

Blue Hole Dive Center
☎ 226-2982
www.bluedive.com
bluehole@btl.net

Bottom Time Dive Shop
☎ 226-2348 fax: 226-2437
www.banyanbay.com
bottomtime@btl.net

Coral Beach Hotel & Dive Club
☎ 226-2817/2013 fax: 226-2864
www.coralbeachhotel.com
forman@btl.net

Exotic Caye Beach Resort
☎ 226-2870
toll-free ☎ 800-201-9389
www.belizeisfun.com
playador@btl.net

Fantasea
☎ 226-2576
www.ambergriscaye.com/fantasea
fantasea@btl.net

Gaz Cooper's Dive Belize
☎ 226-3202
toll-free ☎ 800-499-3002
www.divebelize.com
gaz@btl.net

Hustler Tours
☎ 226-2538/4137 fax: 226-4136
www.scubadivingbelize.net
hustler@btl.net

Larry Parker's Reef Divers
☎ 226-3134 fax: 226-2943
www.reefdivers.com
info@reefdivers.com

Paradise Villas
☎ 226-2822 fax: 414-258-5336
toll-free ☎ 800-451-7776
www.tradewindsparadisevillas.com
belizetradewinds@aol.com

Ramon's Village
☎ 226-2071 or 601-649-1990
fax: 601-649-1996
toll-free ☎ 800-624-4215
www.ramons.com
info@ramons.com

Ambergris Caye (continued)

**The Tides Beach Resort
& Patojo's Scuba Center**
☎ 226-2283 fax: 226-3797
www.ambergriscaye.com/tides
patojos@btl.net

Victoria House
☎ 226-2067 fax: 226-2429
toll-free ☎ 800-247-5159
www.victoria-house.com
info@victoria-house.com

Caye Caulker

Belize Diving Services
☎ 226-0143 fax: 226-0217
www.belizedivingservices.com
bzdiveserv@btl.net

Big Fish Dive Centre
☎ 226-0450

www.bigfishdive.com
bigfishdive@btl.net

Frenchie's Diving Service
☎/fax: 226-0234
www.belizenet.com/frenchies.html
frenchies@btl.net

St. George's Caye

St. George's Lodge
☎/fax: 220-9121
toll-free ☎ 800-678-6871

www.gooddiving.com
info@gooddiving.com

Turneffe Islands

Blackbird Caye Resort
Blackbird Caye
☎ 305-969-7947 fax: 305-969-7946
toll-free ☎ 888-271-3483
www.blackbirdresort.com
dive@blackbirdresort.com

Turneffe Flats
Blackbird Caye
☎ 605-578-1304 fax: 605-578-7540
toll-free ☎ 800-815-1304

www.tflats.com
vacation@tflats.com

Turneffe Island Lodge
Caye Bokel
☎ 713-313-4670 fax: 713-313-4671
toll-free ☎ 800-874-0118
www.turneffelodge.com
info@turneffelodge.com

Lighthouse Reef

Lighthouse Reef Resort
Northern Caye
☎ 223-1205 or 863-439-6600
fax: 863-439-2118

toll-free ☎ 800-423-3114
www.scubabelize.com
larc@tampabay.rr.com

Glover's Reef

Glover's Atoll Resort
Northeast Caye
☎ 520-5016 or 614-8351/7177
www.glovers.com.bz
glovers@btl.net

Isla Marisol Resort
Southwest Caye
☎ 522-0319 or 520-5056
www.islamarisol.com
islamarisol@btl.net

Manta Resort
Southwest Caye
☎ 305-969-7947 fax: 305-969-7946

toll-free ☎ 800-326-1724
www.mantaresort.com
info@mantaresort.com

Off the Wall Dive Shop
Long Caye
☎ 614-6348
offthewall@btl.net

Slickrock Adventures
Long Caye
toll-free ☎ 800-390-5715 fax: 435-259-6996
www.slickrock.com
slickrock@slickrock.com

Dangriga

Hamanasi Dive & Adventure Resort
☎ 520-2073 fax: 520-2090
toll-free ☎ 877-552-3483
www.hamanasi.com
info@hamanasi.com

Second Nature Divers
☎/fax: 523-7038
www.belizediversity.com
divers@btl.net

Tobacco Caye

Tobacco Caye Diving
☎/fax: 614-9907 or 505-710-3678

www.tobaccocayediving.com
info@tobaccocayediving.com

South Water Caye

Blue Marlin Lodge
☎ 522-2243/2759 fax: 522-2296
toll-free ☎ 800-798-1558
www.bluemarlinlodge.com
marlin@btl.net

Pelican Beach Resort
☎ 522-2044 fax: 522-2570
www.pelicanbeachbelize.com
sales@pelicanbeachbelize.com

Placencia

Aquatic Adventures
☎/fax: 523-3182
glenmar@btl.net

The Inn at Robert's Grove
☎ 523-3565 fax: 523-3567
toll-free ☎ 800-565-9757
www.robertsgrove.com
info@robertsgrove.com

Kitty's Place Beach Resort
☎ 523-3227 fax: 523-3226
www.kittysplace.com
info@kittysplace.com

Nautical Inn
☎ 523-3595 fax: 523-3594
toll-free ☎ 800-688-0377
www.nauticalinnbelize.com
nautical@btl.net

Placencia Dive Shop
☎/fax: 523-3313
plaindltd@btl.net

Rum Point Inn
☎ 523-3239/3241 fax: 523-3240
toll-free ☎ 888-235-4031
www.rumpoint.com
rupel@btl.net

Sea Horse Dive Shop
☎/fax: 523-3166
toll-free ☎ 800-991-1969
www.belizescuba.com
seahorse@btl.net

Serenade Island Resort
☎/fax: 523-3481
www.belizecayes.com
serenade@btl.net

Live Aboards

Two live-aboard boats operate in Belizean waters. These are large, comfortable vessels with professional crews that teach a range of certification and specialty courses. Both boats also carry nitrox. The emphasis is on diving, with few shore excursions.

A third vessel, Wave Dancer, from the Peter Hughes fleet, was damaged during Hurricane Iris in October 2001. This boat was scheduled to be replaced by Sun Dancer II in August 2002. For more information, check the Peter Hughes Diving website (www.peterhughes.com).

Belize Aggressor III
Home Port: Belize City
Description: 120ft aluminum monohull
Passengers: 18
☎ 985-385-2628 fax: 985-384-0817
toll-free ☎ 800-348-2628
www.aggressor.com
belize@aggressor.com

Nekton Pilot
Home Port: Belize City
Description: 78ft steel/aluminum multihull
Passengers: 32
☎ 954-463-9324 fax: 954-463-8938
toll-free ☎ 800-899-6753
www.nektoncruises.com
info@nektoncruises.com

Tourist Offices

Belize Tourism Board
New Central Bank Building, Level 2
Gabourel Lane
P.O. Box 325
Belize City
☎ 223-1913 fax: 223-1943
toll-free ☎ 800-624-0686
www.travelbelize.org
info@travelbelize.org

Belize Tourism Industry Association
10 N. Park St.
P.O. Box 62
Belize City
☎ 227-5717 fax: 227-8710
www.btia.org
btia@btl.net

Index

dive sites covered in this book appear in **bold** type

A

Abyss, The 114
accommodations 21-22, 128-132
activities and attractions 23-29
air travel 16
Altun Ha 27-28
Ambergris Caye 42-44
Amigos' Wreck 54-55
Aquarium, The 95
atolls 9, 12, 82-84, 91, 107, 110

B

Bacalar Chico National Park
  & Marine Reserve 34
barracuda 121
batfish 111
Belize Barrier Reef 12, 34, 42-45, 58-60,
  69-71, 124
Belize City 16-18
Belize Zoo 23
Belmopan 11
Bermudian Landing Community
  Baboon Sanctuary 25
Bev's Garden 113
Bird Cayes 37
Black Beauty 90
Black Coral Wall 85
Blue Creek 37
Blue Hole 93-94
Blue Hole Natural Monument 34
boat travel 18
Boca Ciega 51
bristle worm 123
British Honduras 11, 13
business hours 21

C

Caracol 29
cave dive sites 48, 51-52, 88, 93-94, 96,
  113-114
Caye Caulker 42-45
Caye Chapel Reef 57

certification 36
Chub Canyons 81
cleaning station 99
climate 15
Cockscomb Basin Wildlife Sanctuary 26
Colson Cayes 37
Columbus, Christopher 12
Coral Canyons 56
Coral Monument Canyon 68
Cousteau, Jacques 9, 112
Crack, The 113-114
Crooked Tree Wildlife Sanctuary 24
'Cuda Point ('Cuda Scuda) 62
currency *see* money
Cypress Tunnels 51-52

D

DAN (Divers Alert Network) 32
Dangriga 58
day boats 38
dining 22
dive boat evaluation 31
dive resorts 130-132
Divers Alert Network *see* DAN
dive site icons 39
dive training 36
diving and flying 30
diving conditions 15
diving services 130-132

E

Eagle Ray Bowl 66-67
Eagle Ray Wall 37, 94-95
economy 13
Elbow, The 90
electricity 19
Elkhorn Forest 103-104
Emerald Forest 37
entry 19
equipment 20
Esmarelda 50
expertise levels 40

F

Faegon's Bluff 61
Faegon's Point 60-61
faro reef 75
fire coral 123
fire worm *see* bristle worm
Fishy Point 63
food 22

G

Gales Point Wildlife Sanctuary 26
geography 11
geology 12
Gladden Spit 70
Glover's Reef 107-117
Glover's Reef Marine Reserve 34, 110
Guanacaste National Park 26

H

Half Moon Caye Natural Monument 34,
    106
Half Moon Flats 37
Half Moon Wall 104
hazardous marine life 121-123
health 30-33
history 12-13
Hol Chan Cut 37, 53
Hol Chan Marine Reserve 44-45, 53
Hollywood 37
Hopkins 58
hospitals 32-33
HMS *Merlin* 13
hurricane 11, 15, 44

J

Jack Fish City 67
jellyfish 122
Julie's Jungle 98

L

Lamanai 28
language 15
Laughing Bird Caye 37, 74
Laughing Bird Caye National Park 34, 75
Laughing Bird Caye North 73
Laughing Bird Caye South 75-76
Lighthouse Reef 91-107

live-aboards 36, 38, 132
Long Caye 37
Long Caye Cut 111
Long Caye Lagoon 110
Long Caye Ridge 100-101
Long Caye Wall 112
Lubaantun 29

M

malaria 30
manta ray 70
maps
    Belize City 17
    dive site maps
        Glover's Reef 109
        Lighthouse Reef 92
        Middle Cayes 59
        Northern Cayes 43
        Southern Cayes 71
        Turneffe Islands 83
    highlights map 14
    locator map 9
    map index 41
    parks & protected areas 125
marine conservation organizations 127
marine life 118-120
marine reserves 34, 53, 75, 81, 106, 110,
    124-125
Maya Mountains 11, 29
Mayan Empire 12
Mayan ruins 27-29
measurement 20
medical facilities 32-33
Mermaids' Lair 49
Mexico Rocks 37, 45
Middle Caye Wall 114-115
Mini Elbow 86
money 19
moray eel 122
Mosquito Caye 37
Mosquito Caye South 72

N

national park objectives 124
night diving 65
No Cocos (Tres Cocos) 102-103
North Wall 76
Nurse Shark Ridge 102

P

Painted Wall 96
Pete's Palace 101
photography, underwater 20-21
Pillar Coral 52
Pinnacles, The 115-116
Placencia 69-71
Pompion Caye 37, 80
Pompion Caye Wall 79
population 11
pre-trip preparation 31-32

Q

Quebrada 99-100
Queen Cayes (Silk Cayes) 37, 77

R

recompression chamber 33
resorts *see* accommodations
responsible diving 126-127
restaurants *see* dining

S

Sand Bore 37
Sandy Lane 84-85
San Pedro 44
Sapodilla Cayes Marine Reserve 34, 81
Sayonara 88
Scipio Cayes 37
scorpionfish 121
sea urchin 123
shark 121
Shark Point 106
Shark-Ray Alley 37, 54
shopping 22
shore dive sites 56, 64-65, 72, 74, 77, 80, 110
Silk Cayes Canyons 78
Silk Cayes (Queen Cayes) 37, 77
Silver Caves 96
Sittee River 58
snorkeling 36
snorkeling sites 37, 45, 53, 54, 56, 64-65, 72, 74, 77, 80, 93-95, 110-111
South Water Caye 37, 60

South Water Caye Marine Reserve 34
Split, The 37, 44
Statue 46
stingray 122
Stingray Village 37, 56

T

Tackle Box Canyons 48
tax 19
taxis 18
telephone calls 128
time 19
tipping 19
Tobacco Caye 37, 58
Tobacco Channel 66
Tobacco Cut 64-65
tourist offices 132
transportation 18-19
Tres Cocos (Ambergris Caye) 47
Tres Cocos (No Cocos) 102-103
Triple Anchors 87
Turneffe Islands 82-90
Turtle's Rest 64

V

Victoria Peak 11, 26

W

water (drinking) 22
water taxis 18
water temperatures 15
water visibility 15
West Point Wall 88
West Wall 117
whale shark 70
what to bring 20
wreck dive sites 54-55, 87-88

X

Xunantunich 28-29

Lonely Planet Pisces Books

The **Diving & Snorkeling** guides cover top destinations worldwide. Beautifully illustrated with full-color photos throughout, the series explores the best diving and snorkeling areas and prepares divers for what to expect when they get there. Each site is described in detail, with information on suggested ability levels, depth, visibility and, of course, marine life. There's basic topside information as well for each destination.

Also check out dive guides to:

Australia's
Great Barrier Reef

Australia: Southeast Coast

Bali & Lombok

Bermuda

Bonaire

Chuuk Lagoon,
Pohnpei & Kosrae

Cocos Island

Curaçao

Dominica

Fiji

Guam & Yap

Jamaica

Maldives

Monterey Peninsula
& Northern California

Pacific Northwest

Philippines

Puerto Rico

Red Sea

Scotland

Seychelles

Southern California
& the Channel Islands

Tahiti & French Polynesia

Thailand

Texas

Vanuatu